‹ ( ) › human rights *first*

Fixing Bagram

An Examination of the Detention and Trials of Bagram Detainees

November 2009

About Us

Human Rights First believes that building respect for human rights and the rule of law will help ensure the dignity to which every individual is entitled and will stem tyranny, extremism, intolerance, and violence.

Human Rights First protects people at risk: refugees who flee persecution, victims of crimes against humanity or other mass human rights violations, victims of discrimination, those whose rights are eroded in the name of national security, and human rights advocates who are targeted for defending the rights of others. These groups are often the first victims of societal instability and breakdown; their treatment is a harbinger of wider-scale repression. Human Rights First works to prevent violations against these groups and to seek justice and accountability for violations against them.

Human Rights First is practical and effective. We advocate for change at the highest levels of national and international policymaking. We seek justice through the courts. We raise awareness and understanding through the media. We build coalitions among those with divergent views. And we mobilize people to act.

Human Rights First is a non-profit, nonpartisan international human rights organization based in New York and Washington D.C. To maintain our independence, we accept no government funding.

This report is available for free online at
www.humanrightsfirst.org

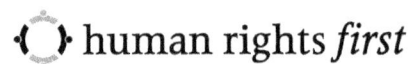

Acknowledgements

These reports were written by Sahr MuhammedAlly, Senior Associate in the Law and Security Program.

They were edited by Gabor Rona, International Legal Director, Tad Stahnke, Director of Policy and Programs, and Elisa Massimino, CEO and President of Human Rights First. Dr. Farouq Samim provided invaluable research and translation assistance. Research assistance was provided by Sofia Rahman, Melissa Koven, Melina Milazzo, and Renée Schomp. Sarah Graham provided production assistance.

Human Rights First would like to thank all those who spoke with us. We are particularly grateful to former Bagram detainees who took the time and effort to travel to Kabul and Jalalabad to share their stories with us. We are grateful to the Afghan Human Rights Organization (AHRO), the Afghan Independent Human Rights Organization (AIHRC), and International Legal Foundation-Afghanistan. We would like to thank officials from the ANDF Review Committee, the Attorney General of Afghanistan, Afghan prosecutors and defense lawyers, Staff Judge Advocate, U.S.-Forces Afghanistan, U.S. Central Command in Tampa, and the Office of Detainee Affairs.

We would also like to thank the International Justice Network.

Human Rights First gratefully acknowledges the generous support of The Atlantic Philanthropies, Bullitt Foundation, John Merk Fund, Open Society Institute, and The Overbrook Foundation.

❮❯ human rights *first*

Headquarters	Washington D.C. Office
333 Seventh Avenue	100 Maryland Avenue, NE
13th Floor	Suite 500
New York, NY 10001-5108	Washington, DC 20002-5625
Tel.: 212.845.5200	Tel: 202.547.5692
Fax: 212.845.5299	Fax: 202.543.5999

www.humanrightsfirst.org

AFGHANISTAN

Glossary

AIHRC	Afghan Independent Human Rights Commission
ANA	Afghan National Army
ANDF	Afghan National Detention Facility
ANP	Afghan National Police
ANSF	Afghan National Security Forces
AUMF	Authorization for Use of Military Force
BTIF	Bagram Theater Internment Facility
CCCI	Central Criminal Court of Iraq
CENTCOM	U.S. Central Command
CJIATF	Combined Joint Interagency Task Force
CSRT	Combatant Status Review Tribunal
DRB	Detainee Review Board
EC	Enemy Combatant
FOB	Forwarding Operating Base
ICRC	International Committee of the Red Cross
ICCPR	International Covenant of Civil and Political Rights
ICPC	2004 Interim Criminal Procedure Code for Courts
IAC	International Armed Conflict
IHL	International Humanitarian Law
IHRL	International Human Rights Law
ISAF	International Security Assistance Force
JTF435	Joint Task Force 435
LLEC	Low Level Enemy Combatant
NATO	North Atlantic Treaty Organization
NDS	National Directorate of Security
NIAC	Non-International Armed Conflict
OEF	Operation Enduring Freedom
POW	Prisoner of War
UECRB	Unlawful Enemy Combatant Review Board
UNAMA	United Nations Assistance Mission in Afghanistan

Table of Contents

Undue Process
An Examination of Detention and Trials of Bagram Detainees in April 2009

Fixing Bagram
Strengthening Detention Reforms to Align with U.S. Strategic Priorities

Undue Process

An Examination of Detention and Trials of Bagram Detainees in April 2009

I. Preface

In response to the September 11 attacks, the United States launched Operation Enduring Freedom (OEF) in Afghanistan to kill and capture "high-value" al Qaeda and Taliban members and destroy the safe havens from which al Qaeda planned and directed the 9/11 attacks. The Taliban government collapsed in November 2001, and the war that the United States is fighting in Afghanistan has changed significantly.

From December 2002, the government of President Hamid Karzai has exercised territorial sovereignty over Afghanistan. Since 2005, insurgent forces have launched armed attacks on the Afghan government, the U.S. military, and the North Atlantic Treaty Organization (NATO)-led International Security Assistance Forces (ISAF), and on the civilian population.[1]

Today, militaries from Afghanistan, the United States, and other countries are operating in a complex environment where the goals include defeating the insurgency and building a stable Afghanistan.

In April 2009, Human Rights First interviewed former prisoners held by the United States in Afghanistan who described how they were captured, treated in U.S.

custody, what they knew about the grounds for their detention, and whether they were able to challenge their detention. The detainees we spoke to were—at the time of their release—found by the U.S. military not to be a threat to U.S., Afghan or Coalition forces. Some detainees we interviewed had been detained for five years, others from four months to two years. Our research also included an assessment of trials of former detainees in Afghan courts.

As of September 2009, around 600 individuals are being held at Bagram Air Base in Parwan province, Afghanistan. Most are Afghans, but an unknown number are non-Afghans. The public does not know their names. Some individuals have been captured outside Afghanistan and brought to Bagram for long-term detention.

According to those we interviewed in April 2009, prisoners held by the U.S. military in Afghanistan were not informed of the reasons for their detention or the specific allegations against them. They were not provided with any evidence that would support claims that they are members of the Taliban, al Qaeda or supporters of other insurgent groups. They did not have lawyers or any other representative to provide them with legal assistance. They could not bring village elders or witnesses to speak on their behalf or offer evidence that the allegations were based on individual animosities or tribal rivalries. These prisoners had no meaningful way to challenge their detention.

As of August 2009, a three-panel military board the Unlawful Enemy Combatant Review Board (UECRB) decided each prisoner's fate based on evidence the prisoner never saw. The options were: continued indefinite detention, release, or transfer to criminal prosecution. Prisoners released by U.S. authorities from Bagram were not given an explanation or apology in the event of wrongful capture. They received a one-page document which stated that the individual, at the time of release, does not pose a threat to U.S. or Coalition forces.

Interviewees who were captured in 2002 and 2003 described being beaten, held in stress positions, threatened with dogs, made to survive on biscuits and water for several weeks, given inadequate food during long-term detention, held in cold isolation cells for several weeks, denied the opportunity to pray or to be provided with water for ablution, and subjected to sleep deprivation at Bagram.

Detainees captured after 2006 described significantly better treatment than those captured earlier, but some still told of being assaulted at the point of capture and being held in cold isolation cells for several weeks after their capture. None, however, reported physical mistreatment during long-term detention in Bagram or interference with their religious practices. However, because no human rights organization or lawyer has access to detainees in Bagram, it is impossible to know the conditions of confinement and treatment of all prisoners at the current time—especially those held in long-term isolation. The International Committee of the Red Cross (ICRC) is the only outside entity allowed to meet detainees, but its findings are confidential and submitted only to the detaining authority.

The United States military states that it retains custody of "high-value" prisoners. But some "low-level" detainees are transferred for prosecution in the U.S.-built Afghan National Defense Facility (ANDF) and are tried under Afghan national security law based on evidence the United States has collected, which may be supplemented by Afghan authorities years after the initial capture. Many have been convicted in proceedings that fail to meet international or Afghan fair trial standards, as there are no witnesses testifying, either in person or by other means, such as by affidavit, during these proceedings.

In contrast to U.S. forces operating under the OEF, ISAF operating in Afghanistan transfer the persons they capture to Afghan custody within ninety-six hours.

The manner in which many of these captures and detentions have been handled in Afghanistan has been counterproductive to U.S. strategy there. Mistaken detentions, ill treatment of detainees, inadequacies in review of the decision to detain, all contribute to diminished support of the United States and its mission in Afghanistan.[2]

Those we interviewed, although not supportive of the Taliban or other insurgent groups, repeatedly cited as reasons for the decline in support civilian casualties, arbitrary detention and ill-treatment, intrusive house searches, the use of dogs against villagers, failure to admit and compensate for losses resulting from personal and property damage as well as from wrongful detention, and cultural insensitivities. Such conduct undermines the cooperation of civilians with the Afghan government and international troops and sends a message that foreign troops are at war with Afghans rather than assisting them.

In May 2009, we submitted our findings and recommendations to the President's Special Task Force on Detainee Disposition, created by Executive Order on January 22, 2009, which was tasked to identify "lawful options. . . with respect to the apprehension, detention, trial, transfer, release, or other disposition of individuals captured or apprehended in connection with armed conflicts and counterterrorism operations, and to identify such options as are consistent with the national security and foreign policy interests of the United States and the interests of justice."[3] We also submitted our findings and recommendations to U.S. Central Command (CENTCOM) and the Department of Defense Office of Detainee Affairs.

In May 2009, at the time of our submissions to the government, we were aware that the Pentagon was revising detainee review procedures in Bagram and that broader detention reforms in Afghanistan were being considered.[4]

In September 2009, the Pentagon made public a new policy guidance for detentions in Afghanistan. The new guidance replaces the Unlawful Enemy Combatant Review Board (UECRB) procedures with new Detainee Review Board (DRB) procedures for detainees being held in the Bagram Theater Internment Facility (BTIF). The new procedures are an improvement from the UECRB, but additional reforms are needed to allow detainees a meaningful way to challenge their detention and to advance U.S. counterinsurgency goals. (For an analysis on the new procedures see *Fixing Bagram: Strengthening Detention Reforms to Align with U.S. Strategic Priorities (Nov. 2009)*).

Our field research in April 2009 provided insight into how and pursuant to what criteria individuals are captured. We also were able to draw conclusions about flaws in the previous UECRB procedures, which failed to provide detainees with a meaningful mechanism to challenge their detention, and defects in the trial of former prisoners in Afghan courts. This report highlights those findings, conclusions, and also lists the recommendations we submitted to the U.S. government in May 2009 as it was undertaking a review of detention reforms.

Human Rights First's recommendations submitted to the U.S. government in May 2009 can be found below in section VI.

* * *

This report is based on research conducted by Human Rights First in Afghanistan in April-May 2009. Human Rights First interviewed former detainees, Afghan defense lawyers and national security prosecutors, the attorney general of Afghanistan, the Afghan National Defense Facility Review Committee, Deputy Staff-Judge Advocate for U.S. Forces Afghanistan, U.S. CENTCOM in Tampa, and officials from the United Nations Assistance Mission in Afghanistan (UNAMA). To protect the identities of former detainees, Human Rights First has used pseudonyms in the form of initials for each interviewee. Some Afghan and U.S. officials did not wish to be identified so their names have been withheld.

II. Detention Operations in Afghanistan

The United States, along with NATO allies and the Afghan government, is engaged in an armed conflict with insurgent groups in Afghanistan. The power to detain is an essential element of armed conflict, serving both the security interest of the detaining authority and the humanitarian interest of the detainee, who might otherwise be killed. There is a complex interplay between legal and practical considerations regarding detention in an armed conflict fought on foreign soil against non-state armed groups. The current U.S. strategy in Afghanistan recognizes the benefits of consent from, and the cooperation of, the local population and authorities in all aspects of the war effort, including detention. Increasing the Afghan stake in detention is already a part of the U.S./ISAF strategy in Afghanistan.

Operation Enduring Freedom

U.S.-led operation Enduring Freedom began on October 7, 2001, four weeks after the September 11 attacks on the United States. OEF's counterterrorism mission has been to capture or kill "high-value" Taliban and al Qaeda members, to destroy the safe havens from which al Qaeda planned and directed the 9/11 attacks, and to eliminate any future safe havens in Afghanistan.

Since June 2009, "U.S. forces Afghanistan" (USFOR-A)—which operate under both OEF and ISAF mandates—are under the command of U.S. Lt. General Stanley McChrystal, who is also the NATO/ISAF commander. Gen. McChrystal reports to both NATO and CENTCOM, which since October 2008 has been led by General David Petraeus. CENTCOM, not NATO, oversees OEF counterterrorism and detainee operations in Afghanistan. OEF and NATO/ISAF missions are separate and, according to U.S. officials, will not formally merge.[5]

Not all agreements between the United States and the government of Afghanistan on military matters are public. All U.S. military forces in Afghanistan operate under a public 2002 diplomatic note between the United States and Afghanistan which authorizes "cooperative efforts in response to terrorism, humanitarian, and civic assistance, military training and exercises, and other activities."[6] The 2002 diplomatic note is silent on detention. The United States occupies Bagram Air Base pursuant to the "Accommodation Consignment Agreement for Lands and Facilities in Bagram Airfield," which allows the United States and coalition forces "exclusive, peaceable, undisturbed and uninterrupted possession" of Bagram, without charge, for military purposes.[7]

According to Col. Charles Tennison, Commander of Detention Operations in 2008, Combined Joint Task Force 101, "the U.S. Armed Forces and allied forces have detained thousands of individuals believed to be members or supporters of either al Qaeda or the Taliban. Since military operations began in Afghanistan, the United States has screened and released many individuals. . . . A small percentage . . . of individuals captured by the United States or transferred to United States control are, or have been, held at the [Bagram Theater Internment Facility]."[8]

A 2004 Pentagon inspection and assessment of U.S. detention operations in Afghanistan concluded that "US detainee operations can only be normalized by the emergence of an Afghan justice and corrections system that can assume the responsibility for the long-term detention of low level enemy combatants currently held by the US."[9] The report continued:

> The value of continuing to keep low-level enemy combatants in custody is simply to keep individuals that represent a proven threat to coalition forces off the battlefield. This is a function that can and should be undertaken by the Afghan government. . . . Despite efforts to improve the process, the press of a growing detainee population without an Afghan solution or continued transfer to GTMO will continue to create the potential for bad choices to be made at several points in that process.[10]

Against this backdrop, in August 2005, the Afghan and U.S. governments entered into a bilateral agreement through an exchange of diplomatic notes (the 2005 Notes) that set forth conditions for the transfer of Afghan detainees in U.S. custody to the Afghan government. The 2005 Notes are not public, but reference to an agreement between the two countries regarding detainees is contained in a U.S. Embassy Kabul press release, dated August 4, 2005:

> Today, in beginning to implement the Joint Declaration on Strategic Partnership, Afghanistan and the United States reached an understanding that will allow for the gradual transfer of Afghan detainees to the exclusive custody and control of the Afghan Government. The Government of Afghanistan will accept responsibility for the returning Afghan citizens and will work to ensure that they do not pose a continuing threat to Afghanistan, the Coalition, or the international community as a whole. The United States is prepared to assist Afghanistan in capacity building, including infrastructure, and to provide training, as appropriate.[11]

According to the *New York Times*, which has obtained a draft of the 2005 Notes, Washington asked Kabul to share intelligence information concerning detainees, to "utilize all methods appropriate and permissible under Afghan law to surveil or monitor their activities following any release," and to "confiscate or deny passports and take measures to prevent each national from traveling outside Afghanistan."[12] For its part, the United States

agreed to finance the reconstruction of an Afghan prison block and help equip and train an Afghan guard force.[13] The Afghan National Defense Facility is the prison block that houses and prosecutes former Guantánamo and Bagram prisoners.

The U.S. and Afghan government also entered into a 2005 Joint Declaration of the United States-Afghanistan Strategic Partnership which provides that the "U.S. military forces operating in Afghanistan will continue to have access to Bagram Air Base and its facilities, and facilities at other locations as may be mutually determined and that the U.S. and Coalition forces are to continue to have the freedom of action required to conduct appropriate military operations based on consultations and pre-agreed procedures."[14] The 2005 Joint Declaration does not provide the United States with its own detention authority but instead addresses detainee operations by the Afghan government: "As Afghan Government capabilities increase . . . the Afghan Government intends to maintain capabilities for the detention, as appropriate, of persons apprehended in the War on Terror."[15]

According to Secretary of Defense Robert Gates, as of January 27, 2009, there were approximately 615 detainees in the Bagram Theater Internment Facility (BTIF).[16] An unknown number of detainees in Bagram have been transferred to Afghanistan from other countries.[17] On January 30, 2009, a Pentagon spokesperson stated that there were 570 detainees in Bagram, including thirty non-Afghans captured either in Afghanistan or taken into custody outside Afghanistan.[18] The Pentagon has not publicly repeated these numbers since January 30. In April 2009, the ICRC stated that it had visited about 550 Bagram detainees, most of whom were Afghan nationals.[19] In 2009, a new detention facility that can hold over 1100 detainees is expected to open in Bagram.[20]

Under the OEF counterterrorism mission and until September 2009, U.S. forces could detain "unlawful enemy combatants" in order to:

[Prevent] them from returning to the battlefield and [deny] the enemy the fighters needed to conduct further attacks and perpetrate hostilities against innocent civilians, U.S. and coalition forces, and the Government of Afghanistan. The United States also gathers important intelligence from the unlawful enemy combatants during their detention, which in turn enables the United States to prevent future attacks.[21]

A September 2006 Pentagon directive defined "unlawful enemy combatant" as:

[P]ersons not entitled to combatant immunity, who engage in acts against the United States or its coalition partners in violation of the laws and customs of war during an armed conflict. For purposes of the war on terrorism, the term Unlawful Enemy Combatant is defined to include, but is not limited to, an individual who is or was part of or supporting Taliban or al Qaeda forces or associated forces that are engaged in hostilities against the United States or its coalition partners.[22]

The 2006 DOD directive also instructs that any detainee in U.S. military custody not granted prisoner of war (PoW) status "shall have the basis for their detention reviewed periodically by a competent authority."[23]

Individuals captured and held in Bagram, under the OEF counterterrorism mandate, were captured and detained according to the above criteria. The basis for capture and detention was modified in mid-September 2009. Under the new criteria, U.S. forces can detain:

Persons who planned, authorized, committed, or aided the terrorist attacks that occurred on September 11, 2001, and persons who harbored those responsible for those attacks.

Persons who were part of, or substantially supported Taliban or al-Qaida forces or associated forces that are engaged in hostilities against the United States or its coalition partners, including any person who has committed a belligerent act, or has directly supported hostilities, in aid of such enemy armed forces.[24]

(See *Fixing Bagram: Strengthening Detention Reforms to Align with U.S. Strategic Priorities (Nov. 2009)*).

Since 2007 and until September 2009, detentions in Bagram were reviewed by the Unlawful Enemy Combatant Review Board.[25] According to Col. Charles Tennison, the Commander of Detention Operations in 2008, Combined Joint Task Force 101, a detainee in Bagram was "notified of the general basis of his detention within the first two weeks of in-processing. . . . [b]arring operational requirements."[26] A review of a detainee's status in Bagram was "usually conducted"[27] within seventy-five days of detention and every six months thereafter. The UECRB, comprised of three commissioned officers, assessed a detainee's status and by majority vote recommended to the Commanding General or his designee that a detainee either be released or remain in detention.[28] The UECRB reviewed information from a "variety of sources, including classified intelligence and testimony from individuals involved in the capture and interrogation of the detainee."[29] Since April 2008, detainees being screened for the first time had an opportunity to appear before the UECRB for their initial review and make written submissions in subsequent reviews.[30] The "implementing guidance" for UECRBs and the documentation prepared for UECRB evaluations of detainees are classified.[31]

The UECRB identified which individuals should be released or transferred to the Afghan-led *Takhim e Sol* national reconciliation process or to Afghan authorities for prosecution. (*See* Appendix B for a copy of a Bagram release document). Individuals nominated for reconciliation are vetted and selected by the *Takhim e Sol* for return to their village elders and reintegration into Afghan society. A number of individuals are also transferred to Afghan custody for prosecution for violations of Afghan national security law at the U.S.-built Afghan National Defense Facility.

A CENTCOM official in May 2008 explained to Human Rights First that while it is not the goal of the United States to keep detainees "any longer than is absolutely necessary . . . for some detainees detention is sometimes the only way to mitigate the threat to U.S. and Coalition forces."[32] The official explained that although the United States is transferring low-level enemy combatants to Afghan authority for prosecution, the United States will retain custody of "higher level combatants" who pose a threat to the United States or coalition forces because the U.S. is better able to "mitigate the threat against our troops."[33]

NATO/ISAF

Most U.S. allies participate in coalition operations in Afghanistan not as part of OEF operations, but as part of ISAF. ISAF operates a counterinsurgency mission and in accordance with the 2001 Bonn Agreement and U.N. Security Council Resolution 1386, is mandated to assist the Afghan government "in the maintenance of security in Kabul and in surrounding areas" under Chapter VII of the United Nations Charter and is allowed to "take all necessary measures to fulfill its mandate."[34] Subsequent resolutions have expanded ISAF's mandate to all of Afghanistan.[35]

ISAF came under NATO control on August 11, 2003. The U.N. Security Council resolutions do not explicitly refer to detention by international military forces. But between 2002 and 2005, ISAF forces turned captured prisoners over to OEF forces. Since late 2005, however, after reports of secret detention, torture and ill-treatment in U.S. detention facilities, European allies became reluctant to transfer detainees to U.S. custody.[36] ISAF instead began to transfer detainees they capture within 96 hours directly to the Afghan security forces who work jointly with ISAF or to the Afghan intelligence agency the National Directorate of Security (NDS).

The Afghan government has begun urging reforms of international military practices in Afghanistan. In a January 10, 2009 letter to NATO headquarters, the Afghan government proposed a Draft Technical Agreement outlining rules of conduct for NATO troops and their coordination with Afghan defense officials.[37] The agreement states that, where necessary, house searches and detention operations be carried out by Afghan national security forces, that "arrests and imprisonment of Afghan nationals for offenses that are unlawful under the laws of Afghanistan, including terrorism" be carried out by Afghan forces, and that nationals detained for committing terrorist acts inside Afghanistan "shall not be imprisoned or otherwise punished without due process of the Afghan legal system."[38] A U.S. military spokesperson said it is unclear whether the proposed agreement governs separate OEF operations in Afghanistan.[39] At this writing, there are no public reports on the current status of the Afghan proposed agreement.

According to LTC Steven Weir, the Deputy Staff Judge Advocate for USFOR-A in April 2009, ISAF forces since 2009 use a document called the "Karzai 12," which is a list of twelve questions that guide issues pertaining to searches and captures, including coordination with local officials.[40] However, whether troops under the OEF mandate will follow the Karzai 12 is unclear. Human Rights First was informed by LTC Weir that ISAF operations are conducted jointly with the Afghan National Army (ANA) or Afghan National Police (ANP). Currently, in ISAF operations "the Afghans are the first ones through the door and they are the ones interacting with the residents," said LTC Weir.[41] Since 2009, ANA units have also begun to accompany OEF troops, including Special Operations units.[42]

III. Detainee Accounts of Capture and Detentions

In April 2009, Human Rights First interviewed fifteen former detainees who at the time of their release were found by the U.S. military not to be a threat to U.S., Afghan or Coalition forces. Some detainees we interviewed had been detained for five years, others from four months to two years. Their captures took place as early as 2003 and as late as November 2007. The detainees we interviewed were released in 2007, 2008, and in March 2009. The youngest detainee we interviewed was twenty-three and the oldest fifty-eight. The accounts below are based on individuals captured and processed through Bagram prior to September 2009 when the new changes were implemented.

Every former detainee we interviewed told us that upon transfer to Bagram, he was not provided with any official (and sometimes not even an informal) statement of the reasons for his detention. All detainees were interrogated, but were not provided with any opportunity to challenge their detention, such as by examining the evidence or given the opportunity to provide evidence or witnesses of their own. Several of the detainees told us that in their opinion dangerous individuals are detained in Bagram, e.g. individuals who have engaged in anti-government activities and are a threat to Afghan and Coalition forces. But this underscores the importance of ensuring that detention decisions are based on reliable information and that there is a meaningful process to review detention decisions for all prisoners in order to ensure that those who are not a threat do not continue to be detained.

Human Rights First did not interview the entire detainee population in Bagram because we do not have access to the facility. But even if we did, the lack of meaningful process described by former prisoners we interviewed is consistent with conclusions of the ICRC and at least one U.S. district judge. The ICRC has expressed concern about the lack of an appropriate legal framework for detentions and the need for more robust procedural safeguards in Bagram.[43] And a U.S. district court judge, upon examination of the UECRB procedures submitted by the government during litigation, has concluded that the Bagram Unlawful Enemy Combatant Review Boards provide even less due process than the discredited Combatant Status Review Tribunals (CSRTs) in Guantánamo.[44]

Detainees recounted abuses in treatment, although the extent of these abuses appears to have diminished after 2006 amongst the individuals we interviewed. The interviews also demonstrate some of the negative impact that U.S. detention operations have had on the willingness of Afghans to cooperate with international forces.

The Capture

None of the individuals we interviewed were captured during a "firefight." They were captured in their homes during a night raid[45] or, in one case, on the way to plough a field, and in the case of one individual while working on a U.S. base. We do not take the occasion of this report to assess, under the laws of war, the rules of engagement of U.S. military forces during a raid or search. We also acknowledge that the interviewees do not constitute the various circumstances of all captures since we don't have access to all Bagram prisoners. Nevertheless, the descriptions by former prisoners provide a factual account of some captures and inform how the military could improve its procedures in this area.

Detainees described being hooded or blindfolded, handcuffed and taken in a vehicle to the nearby airbase or Forward Operating Base (FOB) after their capture. Upon arrival they were held in small wooden isolation rooms and given water, biscuits, or MREs (Meals Ready to Eat). Detainees captured post 2006 were held in the FOB or airbase between three and seven days before being transferred to Bagram, whereas those captured in 2003 and 2004 were held in a FOB for several weeks before being transferred first to Kandahar air base and then to Bagram.

N.K. was captured in 2007 in his home in Khogiani district, on the outskirts of the provincial capital of Jalalabad. He was transferred to Afghan custody one year later, in 2008, and released from the ANDF on April 19, 2009. He described the night of his capture:

> Foreign soldiers entered my house. They used explosives on the door. There was shrapnel created from the explosives which killed the sheep, cows, and goats in the compound. We were all scared and the women and children were hiding. I later learned that the entire village was surrounded and others were captured as well. My older brother and I were captured. Two of my neighbors heard the shouting and gunfire and came to help. I was kicked and punched. . . . There was blood in my urine later that day. . . .I was hooded, handcuffed, and taken in a vehicle to Jalalabad airbase. . . .I was put in a small isolation cell and spent five days there before being taken to Bagram.[46]

M.A., from Nangrahar province, was captured in his home in 2007. He told Human Rights First:

> I was asleep at home and heard the sounds of shooting. I thought maybe there are thieves. I had a mobile phone and 10,000 Pakistani Rupees which I hid in the bushes.[47] The shooting grew louder and louder. We saw that foreigners were coming. . . . They climbed over the walls and pushed the door in and arrested us. . . . First they told me to raise my hands. They searched and handcuffed me. I was pushed and told to lie face down. I was taken to Sarabagh airbase and then later to Bagram.[48]

Twenty-eight-year-old A.M. from Nangrahar province was also captured in his home by U.S. forces around midnight or 1:00 a.m. He told Human Rights First, "We have rivalries with other tribes. I thought someone was breaking into our house so I picked up my gun but my house was completely surrounded so I surrendered."[49]

M.K., from Nangrahar province, who was in U.S. custody for two days and nights in March 2009, was outraged at the raid of his home and his capture:

> The foreign soldiers entered my house, destroyed everything. They broke teapots, glasses, searched under the rugs, mattresses, and damaged them. At the end they did not find a single piece of evidence against me. They found three AK-47s and one pistol, which I have permission to carry from the current government. I had five vehicles inside the compound. One was for me and the others belonged to some elders who had come to the village for a jirga [meeting] and parked their vehicles in my compound. Who gave them the right to burn the vehicles? There was a tractor they burned that too. Why? Even if I was a criminal, were my children and women criminals that they attacked the whole compound? The shooting and raid of my house was traumatic for my family.[50]

In some of these raids, people were injured or killed. Ajmal, who was captured during a raid at his home, told Human Rights First that he learned after his release from Bagram in 2008 that his father had been killed in their home during a subsequent raid. According to press accounts, in 2005, seventy-five-year-old Shayesta Khan was shot dead in his bedroom during a raid on his home by the U.S. military.[51] The raid was prompted by an informant's tip that bombmaking material was in the family compound. But no such material was found. A spokesperson for the U.S. military said that Khan's death was an "unfortunate incident" and U.S. troops returned to the village to offer condolences but insisted that "soldiers violated no rules."[52] According to Afghan officials, U.S. forces acted alone on that particular raid.[53]

K. A. told Human Rights First that his father was shot during a night raid at his home in 2007. "It was 10:00 p.m. My house was surrounded and my house door was broken as soldiers came in. I was captured along with my uncle and relatives who were staying at our house. . . .There were dogs during the raid. My father was sleeping in the yard and was killed when he rose up from his sleep."[54]

On the morning of his capture in November 2007, B.Z. was at a U.S. air base in Oruzgan province. He had been working as a contractor with U.S. Special Forces for some time and was supplying materials for construction.[55] He had been awarded certificates of appreciation from Special Forces. [*See* Appendix C]. While at the base, his satellite phone was taken from him as a security precaution. He was in a room reviewing paperwork when soldiers arrived and accused him of supporting an insurgent group. He was handcuffed and taken to an isolation cell where he spent two days.[56] B.Z. was flown to Kandahar and kept there for an additional two days and then taken to Bagram. He was never shown the evidence against him. During interrogations, he was told that there was suspicious chatter on his satellite phone. He asked to hear the recording of the voices. He asked to see the evidence against him. His requests were denied. B.Z. was released sixteen months later in March 2009.[57]

Fifty-eight-year-old farmer M.I., from Nangrahar province, was detained for nine months. He described how he was captured early one morning on the way to plough his field:

> It was early morning after the call to pray. . . . I had a plough on my shoulders with my two cows. We plough early morning because the weather is good. Along the way, I saw foreign soldiers. I told them that I was going to plough but they arrested me. When Americans first arrested me they did not tell me why. I was yelling and asking why. Through the translator I was told that the Americans were suspicious about me. There was a report about me. I am a simple farmer. I was shaking, I was very scared. I told them if they find that I have done anything wrong then they can execute me. They hand-

> cuffed me, blindfolded me with a piece of cloth . . . . I was pushed, slapped before being put in a vehicle. I was yelling, what is my fault? Why am I being captured? I have never been in such circumstances before.[58]

J.G., from Kunar province, a fifty-four-year-old vegetable street vendor, was captured in 2008 away from his home:

> I was in Jalalabad to sell vegetables as a street vendor. . . .I was leaving the house where I was staying to prepare selling vegetables for the day. It was early morning. As I stepped on the street, I saw foreign troops had surrounded the area. I was arrested and was handcuffed and my eyes were covered. I later learned that there was a raid on a commander's house. I was new to the area so did not know the commander's name. Four or five people were arrested with me.[59]

S.M., from Kunar province, was transporting dynamite for construction of a road and told Human Rights First that he had permits from the provincial and local governments.[60] On the day of his arrest in 2007 by the U.S. military, S.M. was stopped by Afghan police, who demanded a bribe. S.M. told us that when he refused, the police tore up his documents and called the Americans. He was arrested, handcuffed, and taken to Sarabagh base and subsequently to Bagram. According to Shahab he told the interrogators that he had permits to transport the dynamite and could make them available to them because he had copies at home. But there was no way to provide the permits to Bagram authorities. S.M. remained in U.S. custody for fifteen months.[61]

Grounds for Detention

In September 2009, the Pentagon issued a revised policy guidance that changed the name of the class of individuals detainable by OEF forces to "unlawful enemy belligerents." At the time of our interviews in April 2009, under the OEF mandate, U.S. forces could detain an "unlawful enemy combatant" who is "an individual who is or was part of or supporting the Taliban or al Qaeda forces or associated forces that are engaged in hostilities against the United States or its coalition partners."[62]

Former detainees told Human Rights First that they were not informed about the reasons for their detention, other than vague accusations of affiliation with the Taliban, and that they were not shown any evidence to enable them to refute the allegations. Some detainees thought they were captured because they possessed an AK-47, but pointed out that many Afghans who are not affiliated with or supporting insurgent forces possess such weapons to protect themselves and their families.

A.M., who was released after eight months in detention, told Human Rights First,

> I asked [the soldiers] why I was being arrested and they said because I have a gun, that I support the Taliban, and that I was storing weapons for the Taliban. They searched my home and found a gun. Nowadays everyone has one or two guns because we live near the border areas and need it for protection. Most of us don't have permits.[63]

K.H. was captured at age twenty-one, along with his uncle and three of his relatives. His relatives were released the next day but he and his uncle were held for four months. Upon capture, K.H. was asked whether he had brought explosives from Pakistan. "I told them no and to search the house, but there was nothing in my house. . . . In Bagram I was asked questions about what I did, what my uncle did. Had I seen Taliban in the area or seen anyone planting explosives." [64]

The former prisoners we interviewed were all eventually released, having been found not to constitute a threat to the United States. In addition, none of them were prosecuted by Afghan authorities, indicating insufficient evidence of any criminal conduct. They expressed frustration at the lack of investigation prior to a capture or raid on a house to ascertain whether the information is properly sourced and not based on false allegations due to individual animosities and tribal rivalries. Former prisoners told Human Rights First:

- "There is no proper investigation to find out whether the informant is right. America says that someone is a terrorist but maybe the information is given by rivals of that person. In my case I don't know who said what about me that resulted in me being sent to Bagram for four years. Information should be collected from the village, the district, the governor."—A.J., detained for four years.

- "I don't know our [family's] enemy who gave the information to the Americans. The interrogators did not tell us who that person is."—M.A., detained for eight months.

- "Whatever happens is from *Allah*. I don't blame the Americans. People give wrong information. Sometimes people are jealous 'why does he have a good life and not I?' Someone must have complained that I am with the Taliban and al Qaeda. The informant is paid. I told the interrogators [at Bagram] please find one person who made an accusation against me. Ask in my village, the bazaar. If you find that person, I don't want life you can kill me. Ask the Afghan government which family I come from. . . . My whole family is supporting the Karzai government. I am innocent."—B.Z., detained for sixteen months.

- "Someone must have told the Americans that I was working with Taliban. I don't know who that person is and the soldiers never told me. My family must have enemies. I don't know."—K.A., detained for four months.

- "Americans were given information that I was a member of the Taliban and that I was storing weapons and explosives for Taliban. But they did not find any weapons. . . . Information was given based on animosity. I do not know the person who gave the wrong information. I told the Americans to tell me who it was that gave them the information. I told them to go to my village and find out about me. I want to bring people from my village to let the Americans know who I am. But this was not allowed."– S.K., from

Nangrahar province, who was detained for eighteen months.

A cousin of a former detainee suggested that persons who gave misinformation should be punished:

> We don't know who gave the information about my cousin. But Americans know. Why don't they say anything to their spies? Arresting innocent people is creating a strain between the American and Afghan government and the public. This is de-stabilizing. If someone is telling the truth that someone is a militant then he should be rewarded, but if wrong information is given then that agent should be punished publicly for creating problems for innocent Afghans.[65]

An Afghan government official told Human Rights First, "There are lots of tribal rivalries in Afghanistan, people have enemies—sometimes these people will wrongly tell the United States that someone is a Taliban. This results in someone's capture and he is stuck in prison for a long time."[66]

A former detainee who was detained for sixteen months, said:

> Americans are not from my country. They don't know my country. When they arrest someone, go to village, shopkeepers. If 99 percent of them say that the person is innocent then they should not listen to the person who said the opposite. The Americans should ask that maybe this man is saying that I am with the Taliban because he is my rival. Capture people that have done wrong things, but don't arrest innocent people because then they will hold a grudge against you.[67]

J.G., who was fifty when he was captured and held for nine months, said: "When innocent people are captured, people are suspicious of Americans and they want to keep their distance from Americans and will not help them."[68]

M.A., from Nangrahar province, who spent eight months in detention told Human Rights First:

> Americans have come here and they should leave good memories and thoughts in the minds of Afghans. They

should be remembered in a good way. They are guests in our country. But people like us who are innocent and arrested, it's unfair. It is a pity that Americans have left their country and come to our country and doing this to us. Their behavior affects our people and people can turn against the Americans.[69]

In May 2009, the *New York Times* reported on U.S. Captain Kirk Black who, after meeting with a detainee's relatives and local Afghan officials, became convinced that the detainee's detention in Bagram was a case of mistaken identity and put the family in touch with a lawyer.[70] The *New York Times* reported that Captain Black is under investigation concerning his conversations with the detainee's family. In an interview with the *New York Times*, Captain Black said that he was mindful of the dangers of incarcerating someone who might be innocent. "Lock a guy down for 22 hours a day," he said, "and you are creating a criminal."[71]

Collecting and verifying intelligence is challenging in Afghanistan, where tribal rivalries have intensified after thirty years of war and cultural practices make it difficult to discern motives. Civilians are often armed, especially in southern and eastern Afghanistan, where many of the security concerns lie. In accordance with the *Pashtunwali* tribal code, many Afghan villagers will mount a joint defense to an attack on neighbors or the community, regardless of their disdain for the Taliban or support for U.S. forces.[72] In some parts of the country, civilians may be forced to maintain relations with the Taliban and the local government to ensure their own safety.

LTC Steven Weir, Deputy Staff Judge Advocate for U.S. Forces-Afghanistan, acknowledged that NATO, including U.S. forces, are aware of intelligence mistakes and are vetting and verifying human and electronic intelligence collection prior to a raid or capture. "Mistaken identities and captures of wrong individuals. . . based in part due to rivalries is hurting the COIN [counter-insurgency] environment we are operating in," said LTC Weir. But he said that there are also tactical "limitations" because "many Afghans only go by one name and there is no national system for registering" to verify identity. "It would be useful to have a national biometrics database . . . to avoid mistakes in identities," suggested LTC Weir.[73]

New internal directives for ISAF troops implemented in December 2008 instruct that "for ISAF forces to enter a compound there must be two independent sources of intelligence that indicate the targeted individuals in that compound. If Coalition forces do not have the required two sources of intelligence they are only authorized to knock and call out the targeted individual," said LTC Weir.[74]

As discussed above, it is unclear whether OEF troops will rely on "Karzai 12" given the distinct mandates for ISAF and OEF. The use of the "Karzai 12," however, does suggest more Afghan involvement in ISAF and not OEF operations. The requirements for OEF searches of a house or compound are unclear. Human Rights First was informed by LTC Weir that OEF searches are based on "credible intelligence."[75]

Lack of Meaningful Process to Challenge Detention Under the UECRB Procedures

As noted above, an Unlawful Enemy Combatant Review Board examined whether a detainee continues to pose a threat to U.S. and Coalition forces. Human Rights First interviewed several former Bagram detainees who were captured in 2003, 2004, and in November 2007. Some were released in 2007 and others in 2008 and 2009. None of the detainees we spoke to had heard of a "board" reviewing their case, let alone appeared before a review board, including detainees who were in Bagram in 2008 and early 2009, after the UECRB rules had reportedly been amended to allow detainees to appear before the UECRB.

When we asked these former detainees what they were told while in detention, most said that they were told to cooperate, follow orders, not to shout, spit, argue, or hide

food. None of the detainees were informed about the UECRB.

Detainees acknowledged that some individuals in Bagram were threatening the stability of the country and were fighting international troops and the Afghan government, but they urged that there must be a process to distinguish these individuals from those who pose no such threat. The detainees complained that they had no opportunity to counter accusations and were not shown any evidence on which their detention was based, nor were they allowed to bring in tribal elders or individuals from their village who could vouch for them and rebut allegations.

B.Z. from Kandahar expressed sadness at being held for sixteen months in captivity. "I always told them [soldiers in Bagram] that this was a strange justice system that I was in the same cage as someone who had done a lot of bad things. I am educated but what about those who are not and can be influenced by criminals. My heart is burning. I have not done anything wrong. This really hurts me."[76]

Before April 2008, detainees were not permitted to appear before the UECRB. Under the UECRB a detainee was not made aware of the evidence the United States was relying on to justify detention and therefore was deprived of a meaningful way to rebut the basis of detention. Detainees were not permitted to question government witnesses or to call their own witnesses. Bagram detainees do not have access to counsel or a personal representative and have no right to appeal a UECRB determination.[77]

The ICRC has consistently called for the establishment of an appropriate legal framework for detentions in Bagram and emphasized that the development of the UECRB review system "does not mitigate the need for more robust procedural safeguards at Bagram Theater Internment Facility (BTIF)."[78]

In September 2009, the Pentagon made public a new policy guidance on detentions in Afghanistan and replaced the UECRB with the Detainee Review Board procedures. Under the new guidelines, detainees will have improved notification procedures, will be able to attend the hearings, call witnesses who are "reasonably available," question government witnesses, and have a personal representative to assist them during the proceedings. The new procedures are an improvement from the UECRB, but additional reforms are needed to allow detainees a meaningful way to challenge their detention. (For analysis of the new procedures, see *Fixing Bagram: Strengthening Detention Reforms to Align with U.S. Strategic Priorities (Nov. 2009))*.

Treatment and Conditions of Confinement

Between 2002 and 2005, at least two detainees were tortured to death in Bagram and many others were subject to ill-treatment during detention.[79] Neither the United Nations Assistance Mission in Afghanistan (UNAMA) nor the Afghan Independent Human Rights Commission (AIHRC), which is mandated by the Afghan constitution to monitor detention facilities in Afghanistan, nor any other international human rights organization, has access to U.S. detention facilities in Afghanistan. The ICRC is the only non-governmental entity that is permitted access to Bagram and to individual detainees. However, the ICRC maintains a general policy of confidentiality, so details of its findings are not publicly known. Afghan government officials have been given limited access to some Afghan detainees held at Bagram.

Human Rights First interviewed fifteen former Bagram detainees who were captured between 2003 and November 2007. Detainees captured in 2003 and 2004 described being beaten, held in stress positions, threatened with dogs, made to survive on biscuits and water for several weeks, given inadequate food during long-term detention, held in cold isolation cells for several weeks, not allowed to pray or receive water for ablution, and subjected to sleep deprivation in Bagram.

G.K. was sixteen when he was captured in late 2003 in his home in Khost. He was detained for five years—four in U.S. military custody and then transferred to the ANDF for eight to nine months. He was released in late 2008. He described his initial days of capture:

> I was young then. . . .They asked me a lot of questions. . . . . It was the most difficult time of my life. No one would treat even a donkey like the way I was. I was beaten both by U.S. soldiers and Afghan translators. An Afghan would hold my head and the U.S. soldiers put their shoes on my face when I did not want to talk. My hands were tied in front of me and I was chained to a concrete floor and wore goggles for a month. There was something put in my mouth to keep it shut. When I was asked questions they would take it out. For a month I survived on biscuits. When I was allowed to eat, they would take off the handcuffs. During interrogations they would show me maps but I don't know military maps. They would take me to the toilet with my hands tied. My legs were almost paralyzed because they would make me stand for hours. If I fell asleep while standing they would wake me up. They played loud music. My ears hurt. It was hard to sleep. They beat me and shouted at me.[80]

A.B. was captured in his home in Khost in 2004. He told Human Rights First that he was beaten, threatened with dogs, deprived of water to clean himself, held in isolation for several months, and denied natural light for over six months.[81]

> I was in an isolation room. I would beg to be taken to the toilet but the soldiers did not reply to my request. When I was taken to the toilet, I was blindfolded. . . . We were not given toilet paper or water. Urine splashed on my clothes. I was not given a clean set of clothes for nearly a month. I asked for water and was given a small pot of water and five minutes to clean myself but it was not enough. My clothes became dirty and stiff and smelled. I am not exaggerating. This is what I went through.[82]

Bagram Habeas Litigation

In addition to the many Bagram detainees captured in Afghanistan, there are several who were captured outside Afghanistan and brought to Bagram for detention. The individuals captured abroad may well be differently situated in law, as well as in fact, from persons captured locally.

Four Bagram prisoners, nationals of Yemen, Tunisia, and Afghanistan who were reportedly taken into custody in Pakistan, Thailand, and the United Arab Emirates (UAE) and then transferred to Bagram, have filed habeas corpus petitions in the District Court of the District of Columbia. They allege that they have been held for six years or more. According to their individual habeas petitions, Fadi al Maqaleh, a Yemeni citizen, alleges he was taken into U.S. custody sometime in 2003. Haji Wazir, an Afghan citizen, alleges he was captured in Dubai in 2002. Amin al Bakri is a Yemeni citizen, captured by U.S. forces in Thailand in 2002. Redha al-Najar is a citizen of Tunisia and alleges he was captured in Pakistan in 2002.[83]

Oral arguments were held on January 7, 2009. Judge John Bates ordered the government to disclose by January 16th the number of people held at Bagram, how many of them were taken into custody outside of Afghanistan, and how many of the detainees are Afghan nationals. The Justice Department filed a response to the order in which details of detainee numbers, nationalities, or where they were originally taken into custody were redacted from the unclassified version of the filing.[84]

On April 2, 2009, Judge Bates, applying the landmark Supreme Court case *Boumediene v. Bush*, which recognized habeas rights for Guantánamo detainees, ruled that three non-Afghan detainees captured outside Afghanistan and brought to Bagram can challenge the lawfulness of their detention in U.S. federal courts. In the case of Afghan petitioner Wazir, Judge Bates concluded that there was a "possibility of friction with Afghanistan" should Wazir obtain habeas review in U.S. courts. Judge Bates delayed his ruling on the case until further arguments could be made by the parties.[85] The government filed an interlocutory appeal on April 10th and a stay of proceedings was granted on June 1st.[86] On June 26, Judge Bates affirmed the motion to dismiss Haji Wazir's petition.[87]

Judge Bates, in the April 2009 decision, took the view that the UECRBs afforded Bagram detainees were "plainly less sophisticated and more error-prone" than the flawed CSRTs for Guantánamo detainees. Judge Bates concluded that "it suffices to recognize that the UECRB process at Bagram falls well short of what the Supreme Court [in the *Boumediene* case] found inadequate at Guantánamo."[88] Judge Bates also expressed concern that a detainee has no "meaningful opportunity to rebut [the government's] evidence" and that the "ever-changing definition of enemy combatant, coupled with uncertain evidentiary standards, further undercut the reliability of the UECRB review."[89] On September 14, 2009, the Department of Justice filed its brief in the Court of Appeals appealing Judge Bates' decision. Attached to the brief contained the Pentagon's new policy guidance for detentions in the BTIF which replaced the UECRB procedures with the Detainee Review Board procedures. The new procedures were implemented in mid-September 2009.

Detainees captured between 2006 and November 2007 told Human Rights First that although some were assaulted during their capture they were not physically mistreated while in Bagram.

N.K., who was captured in 2007 and claims that he was punched during the capture but not at Bagram, said:

> A Muslim should not lie. I was beaten when I was captured. I was punched in the stomach. But when I was in Bagram there was no torture. The interrogators screamed at me and showed their anger. Sometimes they would hit the table or the box in the room or throw a bottle at the wall. Sometimes the translator would call me "mother fucker" or "pimp."[90]

Most detainees found it humiliating—an offense to their personal dignity—to strip in front of soldiers and take collective showers. M.I. told Human Rights First that he felt "humiliated" when he had to go to the toilet and take showers in front of soldiers and other prisoners.[91] Another detainee said that the "interrogators were respectful" but he characterized being stripped naked as "inhuman" and offensive to his dignity.[92]

Detainees captured in 2003 and 2004, who described abusive treatment during their initial capture, told Human Rights First that during the later years of detention they were not subjected to physical abuse. G.K. told Human Rights First that "they stopped the physical abuse but they shouted and got angry at us."

Detainees captured post 2006 described being held in cold isolation cells after their initial capture. Some detainees we spoke with were in isolation for twenty days, others for longer periods. N.K., who was captured in 2007, told Human Rights First:

> I was held in two different windowless isolation cells for over fifty nights. I was given one blanket but the air conditioning was strong. It was very cold. The light was on constantly. There was a continuous noise which would never stop. Sometimes soldiers would kick the door and shout. It was difficult to sleep. . . . When I was in isolation I did not eat and drink much and became

> weak because I could not go to the bathroom when I wanted. I was not allowed to shower until after twenty-five days of capture. I would think about my family—especially my three-month-old son. . . . It was a difficult time for me.[93]

Detainees captured between 2006 and November 2007 described being interrogated several times during the first month of capture. Sometimes there were two to three interrogations a night and sometimes none for several days. Detainees complained that they could not sleep much during the first month of their capture because of nightly interrogations. They also were held in cold isolation rooms with bright lights, and there was a constant noise echoing in the cells that made sleeping difficult. Detainees told Human Rights First that interrogations became infrequent a couple of months after their capture.

Some former detainees told Human Rights First that detainees who did not obey the rules or who protested the quality of food were punished and taken to cold isolation cells. G.K. described being in an isolation room: "I was in the isolation room as punishment. The air-conditioning was turned up high. I was given no blanket. . . . It was freezing. Our prison uniforms are of thin material."[94] Detainees captured in 2003 and 2004 also stated that when they protested against the quality of food, or made other complaints, guards used "gas" in the cells that made the "eyes watery."[95]

A.B., a former Bagram prisoner captured in 2004, told Human Rights First that prisoners have attempted suicide "but soldiers keep a close watch and it was difficult to know if any prisoner killed himself because he could be in an isolation cell and soldiers are always watching."[96] G.K., who was sixteen when he was captured in 2003, did attempt suicide. "A prison is a prison. It was never easy for me. . . . Whenever I thought of my family I would get upset and wanted to kill myself." G.K. said that he was punished when he attempted suicide:

> My arms and legs were stretched apart and strapped and my head was in a brace against the back of the chair. I was punished like this four to five times. It de-

pends on soldiers how long they kept you. Sometimes eight hours sometimes two days. They would take you to the toilet but not for six to eight hours.[97]

Detainees spoke of having contact with their families through letters transmitted by the ICRC. Some detainees noted that parts of letters from family members were redacted. Since January 2008, Bagram detainees are able to communicate with family members for twenty minutes by means of a video call system, which was set up by U.S. authorities after prolonged negotiations with the ICRC.[98] Since September 2008, families have been allowed to meet their detained relatives face-to-face at BTIF in a new visitation center set up by U.S. authorities. Families register for such visits at the ICRC delegation in Kabul.[99]

Detainees held in communal cells in Bagram in 2008 told Human Rights First that they were given a choice of books to read which were periodically changed. While in communal cells detainees were given a Quran and allowed to pray.

Our detainee interviews suggest an improvement in conditions and treatment after 2006. But given the lack of access to prisoners by independent human rights organizations, it is impossible to assess the current conditions of confinement and interrogation techniques, in particular the impact of long-term detention, and especially on those being held in isolation rather than in communal cells. Moreover, according to the *New York Times*, a 2007 ICRC memorandum found that dozens of Bagram detainees were held in isolation without notification to the ICRC for as long as several months and that some had been subjected to cruel treatment during interrogations.[100] These ICRC findings were made despite changes in detainee treatment policy instituted pursuant to the 2005 Detainee Treatment Act and the 2006 Army Field Manual.[101]

Psychological Harm, Loss of Property and Honor

Released detainees complained of seizure and destruction of property during house raids, lost earning capacity during detention, physical and psychological harm to themselves and their families, and harm to their honor and reputation in the community. Detainees complained that they were released without an apology or any offer of compensation for damaged property, lost earnings, and lost honor.

J.G., who was fifty when he was captured and held for nine months, said:

> Detention is very difficult. I was mentally affected thinking of my children and family. It's hard for me to remember everything. I get bad headaches and take blood pressure medicine every night. Whatever I experienced it came from Allah. That was my destiny. Maybe I deserved it. When I touch my ear, there is a sound in my ear. This is because when I was captured I was beaten.[102]

I.M, from Nangrahar province, who was detained for nine months, said:

> It was very difficult for me to be away from my family when I was in Bagram. Being in detention gave me mental illness. I was concerned about my children. When I remembered them during detention I would get very upset. Now if someone says anything to me that I don't agree with I get angry. Sometimes I want to beat them. I can't control myself. I used to be patient and now I am not. . . . During different periods of war I told my family that we will stay in Afghanistan and will not become refugees. We will die in Afghanistan. We are Pushtuns and want to protect our dignity. Dignity is more important to us than anything else.[103]

Some detainees informed Human Rights First that money seized at the time of capture was returned to them when they were released. Others complained that money hidden in their homes at the time of the raid went missing or their cattle were killed, or vehicles burned and it was difficult to claim compensation for their losses. The U.S. military offers discretionary *solatia* and condolence payments on a case-by-case basis in instances of death and injury and for large-scale damage to individual or community property.[104] None of the individuals we interviewed received any compensation for loss of property.

Former detainees were mindful that there are security problems in Afghanistan and foreign assistance and troops are needed to help the Afghan government, but, in their view, mistakes have been made, lives have been destroyed, and significant economic, mental, and psychological harm is routine.

IV. Trials of Bagram Detainees in Afghan Courts

There continue to be serious problems with conditions of detention, treatment, and trials under Afghan authority. So there can be no simple solution in merely transferring detainees from U.S. to Afghan control. At this writing, Human Rights First is not aware of mistreatment of detainees transferred from U.S. custody to the ANDF. There, are however, public reports of ill-treatment of detainees in Afghan intelligence (NDS) facilities.

Detention is an essential element in armed conflict, and the ultimate goal remains for Afghans to assume responsibility for lawful detentions of Afghans, as well as other aspects of national security. As the United States improves its detention practices, it should continue to assist the Afghan government, as part of its rule of law reform activities, in the improvement of Afghan detention and trial practices, in order to enable Afghanistan to take over responsibility for detention operations.

Immediate improvements in the vetting of U.S. intelligence and evidence gathered at point of capture will both reduce erroneous detentions and improve the credibility of Afghan prosecutions of individuals that the U.S. transfers to them– objectives that will advance U.S. counterinsurgency and rule of law efforts.

In 2007, the United States began transferring some detainees designated as "low-level enemy combatants" to Afghan custody in the U.S.-built Afghan National Defense Facility in Pul-e-Charkhi prison for prosecution. The transferees include detainees from Guantánamo and Bagram. Human Rights First observed trials of former detainees transferred from U.S. custody to the ANDF and in April 2008 issued a report, *Arbitrary Justice: Trials of Bagram and Guantánamo Detainees in Afghanistan*, concluding that the trials fall far short of international and Afghan fair trial standards. Based on a review of the evidence and trial observations, we found that the prosecutions were based on allegations and evidence provided by the United States, supplemented by investigations conducted by the Afghan intelligence agency (NDS), years after the initial capture. Although lawyers defend detainees at the ANDF, during the trials there were no prosecution witnesses, no out-of-court sworn prosecution witness statements, and little or no physical evidence presented to support the charges.[105]

In a civil law system such as Afghanistan's, witness testimony is taken by the investigative prosecutor during the investigation phase and both prosecutor and defense counsel can present and question witnesses at trial.[106] Under the Afghan criminal procedure code, defense counsel and the accused are entitled to be present during witness testimonies at the investigation phase.[107] But this right cannot be exercised where investigations are conducted by the United States prior to the transfer of an individual to Afghan custody and where Afghan defense lawyers are appointed only after follow-up investigations have been completed by Afghan officials and the case has been referred for trial.

In a follow-up visit to Afghanistan in April 2009, Human Rights First met with defense lawyers, a national security prosecutor, the ANDF review committee appointed by President Karzai in March 2008 to assess whether detainees should be released or referred for prosecution, and with the Attorney General of Afghanistan. According to Afghan government sources, as of April 2009 around 200 individuals transferred from U.S. to Afghan custody have been convicted.[108]

The review committee examines the file of each detainee and determines whether any crimes have been committed under Afghan law and, if there is evidence, refers the case for prosecution.[109] Defendants are tried under the 1987 Law of Crimes Against Internal and External Security of the Democratic Republic of Afghanistan (Internal and External Security Law). Detainees are charged with crimes such as destruction of government and private property by explosives (article 5)—punishable by ten to twenty years; organizing activity against the internal and external security (article 9)—punishable by life sentence; and assisting the enemy forces (article 23)—which carries a sentence not exceeding ten years.

The ANDF Review Committee informed Human Rights First that, depending on the evidence in the file and length of time already spent by a prisoner in U.S. custody, a longer prison term might not be warranted and the case might not be referred for prosecution. The committee explained that this may be the result when there is not much evidence in the files or when a prisoner is alleged only to have been caught with one or two AK-47s and he has already spent two to three years in prison.

Prisoners accused of possession of explosives or in possession of a larger number of weapons will be referred for prosecution.[110] The committee expressed concern that, on occasion, a prisoner's file is transferred for review to the committee but the prisoner is not transferred. These prisoners can continue to be detained in Bagram even though the committee has reviewed the file and determined that the individual need not be referred for prosecution and can be released.[111]

At this writing, ten defense lawyers are representing over 300 individuals at the ANDF. Trials are generally between forty-five minutes and an hour in length. Defense lawyers told Human Rights First that the main problem with the trials since they began in 2007 is the absence of prosecution witnesses or even out-of-court sworn witness statements, which makes it difficult to challenge the government's version of events and deprives the defendant of the right to challenge the evidence against him.

A national security prosecutor admitted that there are deficiencies in the evidence but he explained that this is because people were captured several years before their case was prepared for prosecution by the Afghan government.[112] He elaborated, "The Americans are trying to provide us more information, but many times significant evidence is missing. We are not given the weapon or explosives. We then conduct our investigation and then decide whether to prosecute."[113]

Attorney General of Afghanistan Mohammed Ishaq Aloko, who headed the ANDF review committee before being appointed as the attorney general in the fall of 2008, voiced similar concerns about the evidence:

> These people were captured a long time ago and we Afghans don't have all the information. There are tribal, political, and ethnic rivalries. People give wrong information sometimes. We have a difficult time identifying the innocent from the guilty. When we ask detainees questions they claim they are innocent but then if all are innocent then who is carrying out terrorist attacks?[114]

Aloko told Human Rights First that his office "has a good relationship" with the Americans and "together we are trying to find solutions to the problems." He suggested that more lawyers are needed to help process files in Bagram and the ANDF.[115]

Rule of Law and Detention Reform

After thirty years of conflict, the formal Afghan justice sector is weak and faces serious difficulties, including poor infrastructure, inadequate training and education of lawyers and judges, lack of access to laws and textbooks, and corruption. According to the 2007 United Nations Human Development Report, only about one-half of the judges have the relevant formal higher education.[116] The United Nations Assistance Mission in Afghanistan conducted an extensive study of the Afghan justice system and concluded that arbitrary detention is widespread and lengthy pre-trial detentions beyond what is permitted under Afghan law remains a problem.[117] Trials rarely met Afghan or international fair trial standards and administration of justice varied in different parts of the country.

Individuals held by the NDS are subjected to ill-treatment and held arbitrarily. The United Nations High Commissioner for Human Rights concluded that "The [NDS is] responsible for both civil and military intelligence, operates in relative secrecy without adequate judicial oversight and there have been reports of prolonged detention without trial, extortion, torture, and systematic due process violations."[118] A classified presidential decree reportedly sets out the NDS' mandate. In practice, the NDS exercises broad powers of detention, interrogation, and investigation of persons alleged to have committed crimes against national security.[119]

Human Rights First is also aware of concerns that prisons play a role in radicalizing prisoners which further underscores the need to process prisoners expeditiously, house prisoners in humane conditions, ensure fair trials, and to institute vocational training programs to help reintegrate prisoners into society. The United States, along with other countries, is working with Afghanistan to build civilian and military institutions and is the lead donor on rule of law issues, but analysts urge that more resources and coordination on rule of law reform is needed.[120] U.N. Security Council resolution 1833 also stresses the need for the international community to reconstruct and reform prisons in Afghanistan and improve human rights practices and the rule of law.[121]

Human Rights First also learned that when an individual is acquitted by the trial court, he will not be released; rather, the case is automatically sent to the Supreme Court for review pursuant to a 2008 Supreme Court decree.[122] In practice, the final decision on whether an acquitted person will actually be released from the ANDF remains with the attorney general, even after the highest court of Afghanistan has affirmed the acquittal. When Human Rights First asked Attorney General Aloko about such government interference with the judiciary he did not refute it and simply stated that "we are in an emergency situation."[123]

International military troops are concerned that some individuals that they transferred to Afghan custody under ISAF rules were quickly released and re-engaging in anti-government activities. The press has reported that individuals affiliated with the Taliban have broken out or bribed their way out of NDS and other prisons.[124] To date, there have been no such reported incidents regarding the ANDF.

U.S. CENTCOM is concerned about the capacity of the Afghan government to "mitigate threats against U.S. and coalition forces."[125]

An Afghan national security prosecutor acknowledged that the Afghan government's capacity on rule of law issues needs to improve: "Our infrastructure and courts were destroyed due to the wars. It has taken time for the Afghan government to have functioning prisons, courts, police, and army. We are moving forward and we need resources and assistance to build our country. We want to be like other countries with better prisons, investigations, courts, and to protect the human rights of our people."[126]

Human Rights First supports the transfer of detainees to the Afghan authorities where there is evidence of a crime. However, it is critical that, upon transfer, trials meet international fair trial standards. The Afghan government has a legal obligation under Afghan and international law to ensure that persons tried for crimes are informed of and given the opportunity to challenge the evidence. The United States government is encouraging criminal prosecution in Afghan courts, and should take steps to support legitimate prosecutions by shoring up evidence it has collected in connection with capture and detention in order to assist the Afghan government in conducting fair and credible prosecutions.

The United States military has undertaken such efforts in Iraq, where Task Force 134 helped prepare cases of suspected insurgents for prosecution in the Central Criminal Court of Iraq (CCCI). U.S. soldiers have appeared as witnesses in Iraqi courts, even through videoconference, and U.S. judge advocates have trained soldiers and marines in collecting evidence to be used for prosecutions in Iraqi courts.[127]

V. Legal Standards

The United States, along with the Afghan government and NATO allies, is fighting insurgent groups in an armed conflict in Afghanistan. Detention is an essential element of armed conflict, although the legal framework for detention varies depending on whether the armed conflict is considered to be international or non-international in character.[128] But regardless of the source of legal authority for detention, there are applicable principles and standards of international law that provide the floor below which U.S. detention policies and practices must not fall. Current U.S. detention policies and practices do not meet these standards, and must be remedied.

The international armed conflict between the United States and Afghanistan started on October 7, 2001, with U.S. air attacks on Afghanistan. On that date, the four Geneva Conventions of 1949 to which Afghanistan and the United States are party became applicable in their entirety, as did the residual body of customary international humanitarian law applicable to international armed conflict (IAC).[129] Although international human rights law (IHRL) applies at all times to all armed conflicts,[130] relatively few of its specific rules apply to the international armed conflict between two or more states. This is because IHL, as the *lex specialis*, contains detailed rules governing the use of force, the power to detain/right to challenge detention, and the trials and treatment of detainees in such conflicts.

The international armed conflict between the United States and Afghanistan concluded with the inauguration of Hamid Karzai on June 19, 2002, following his election by an Afghan *loya jirga*, to the presidency of the transitional administration of Afghanistan.[131] At this time, the hostilities involving international military forces and

Afghan forces against the Taliban and al Qaeda became a non-international armed conflict (NIAC) governed by the IHL of NIAC, which is codified in Common Article 3 of the Geneva Conventions and Additional Protocol II.[132] The ICRC has concluded that, since June 2002, the war in Afghanistan is a non-international armed conflict.[133]

IHL applicable to international armed conflict authorizes internment of "combatants" to prevent their further participation in hostilities. Internment of "civilians" is authorized "only if the security of the Detaining Power makes it absolutely necessary."[134] IHL applicable to NIAC presumes that the parties can engage in detention, but the contours of that detention are shaped according to domestic law. This is because members of non-state armed groups in NIAC do not enjoy a privilege of belligerency; unlike combatants in an international armed conflict, their hostile acts can be designated as criminal under domestic law.[135] Put another way, NIAC fighters are not entitled to PoW status or treatment; indeed, there is no such thing as PoW status in NIAC. In these situations, civilians who engage in hostilities can either be detained as security threats or criminally prosecuted for their hostile conduct under domestic law.[136]

In the context of the current non-international armed conflict in Afghanistan, the grounds on which such individuals may be detained, and the process to which they are entitled, must be established in law that sets forth relevant grounds and procedures. The ICRC has explicitly affirmed this requirement.[137]

Consistent with international law and with the U.S. strategy to progressively devolve responsibility for detentions to the Afghan government, these grounds and procedures should be addressed through Afghan legislation or if it suffices under the Afghan Constitution, a security agreement between the Afghan and U.S. governments. The grounds and procedures established must be consistent with international humanitarian law and the applicable standards of international human rights law, as outlined below. The implementation of such an agreement regularizing U.S. detention in this way would advance the credibility of U.S. military actions in the eyes of Afghans, thus supporting U.S. counterinsurgency goals in Afghanistan.

The position of the United States on the legal character of the conflict in Afghanistan after the defeat of the Taliban government remains unclear. As discussed below, however, our recommendations for improvements in the legal framework and, in particular, the specific grounds for detention and procedures to challenge the legality of detention are also based on sound policy that reflects American values and interests, and will advance U.S. strategy in Afghanistan, regardless of the administration's view on the legal character of the current conflict. In our view, the United States is obligated to take these steps.[138]

The Authorization for Use of Military Force is an insufficient basis under IHL for detention by the United States in Afghanistan.[139] Passed by Congress in response to the 9/11 attacks, the AUMF authorizes the president to "use all necessary and appropriate force against those nations, organizations, or persons he determines planned, authorized, committed, or aided the terrorist attacks that occurred on September 11, 2001."[140] It does not mention detention and fails to provide procedures for detainees to challenge detention, as required under the IHL of NIAC.[141] Moreover, the AUMF could no more provide a basis for detention by the U.S. in Afghanistan—especially now when the conflict is a non-international one—than could an Afghan law authorize detention of Americans in the U.S.

The ICRC has stated that "[p]ersons detained in relation to a non-international armed conflict waged as part of the fight against terrorism—as is the case in Afghanistan since June 2002—are protected by Article 3 common to the Geneva Conventions and the relevant rules of customary international humanitarian law. The rules of international human rights and domestic law also apply to them. If tried for any crimes they may have committed they are entitled to the fair trial guarantees of international humanitarian and human rights law."[142]

Common Article 3 and Additional Protocol II do not provide procedural guidelines to govern reviews of detention in non-international armed conflicts. Thus it is necessary to refer to human rights law for guidance. The ICRC has similarly stated that Common Article 3 and Additional Protocol II "provide no further guidance on what procedure is to be applied in cases of internment . . .[thus] the gap must be filled by reference to applicable human rights law and domestic law, given that IHL rules applicable in non-international armed conflicts constitute a safety net that is supplemented by the provisions of these bodies of law."[143]

The United States and Afghanistan are both party to the International Covenant of Civil and Political Rights (ICCPR), which prohibits arbitrary detention and mandates court review of any detention.[144] Article 9(4) of the ICCPR states: "Anyone who is deprived of his liberty by arrest or detention shall be entitled to take proceedings before a court, in order that that court may decide without delay on the lawfulness of his detention and order his release if the detention is not lawful."[145]

Article 4 of the ICCPR does permit a state to derogate from its obligations under the Covenant in time of a "public emergency that threatens the life of the nation" and when it "is officially proclaimed."[146] But derogation is never permitted from certain rights, such as the right to life (article 6) and the right to be free from torture and other cruel, inhuman or degrading treatment (article 7).[147] The U.N. Human Rights Committee has interpreted the right to challenge the lawfulness of detention (article 9) to be non-derogable as it is an essential safeguard against torture and other cruel, inhuman or degrading treatment.[148]

The ICRC has developed a set of principles and safe-guards which "reflect the official position of the ICRC" governing security detention in armed conflict and situations of violence.[149] The guidelines "are based on IHL, human rights treaties [such as the ICCPR], and human rights jurisprudence."[150] According to the guidelines, detainees in non-international armed conflict must have the right: to challenge the lawfulness of their detention, have an independent and impartial body decide on continued detention or release, to notice of charges, to a legal representative, to attend hearings, to have contact with family members, and to have access to medical care.[151]

Regardless of whether or not detention authority is deemed to be inherent in the law of war for NIAC, it is clear that the laws of war fail to articulate the permissible grounds and procedures for detention thereby warranting reference to human rights law. This is the situation now extant in Afghanistan and it must be remedied.

Finally, there is the question of sound policy. Our military leaders understand that in a counterinsurgency conflict, the support of the local population is crucial. No one we know disagrees with the conclusion of Defense Secretary Robert Gates and General David Petraeus that "we cannot kill or capture our way to victory."[152] Instead, we submit that the 2007 Rule of Law Manual that accompanies the Counterinsurgency Manual is correct: the United States must hew to generally accepted human rights principles, whether legally mandated or not.[153] We believe they are mandated. Others may have a different view. In the end, adhering to the view that in NIAC, grounds for detention and procedures to challenge it should be embedded in the domestic law of the country of detention is consistent with American justice values, and with the United States' investment in promoting good governance, rule of law, and larger counterinsurgency goals in Afghanistan.

VI. Recommendations

The following recommendations were submitted by Human Rights First to the U.S. government in May 2009.

Detention in a non-international armed conflict, such as in Afghanistan, must be grounded in domestic law, which meets substantive and procedural due process standards of international human rights law.

The Afghan government retains formal sovereignty over its territory, including with respect to persons detained by international military forces operating in Afghanistan. An appropriate legal framework to govern detention operations is necessary to ensure that both international and Afghan military forces are operating within the rule of law in Afghanistan. The Authorization for Use of Military Force (AUMF) passed in response to the 9/11 attacks does not explicitly mention detention and does not provide for the substantive grounds or the procedural due process standards for detention. More importantly, the AUMF could no more provide a basis for detention in Afghanistan than could an Afghan law authorize detention of Americans in the U.S.

The "domestic law" to govern any U.S. detentions could presumably take the form of a security agreement or Afghan legislation which must be approved by the National Assembly of Afghanistan, in accordance with Article 90 of the Constitution of the Islamic Republic of Afghanistan and must comply with the International Covenant of Civil and Political Rights (ICCPR), which prohibits arbitrary detention and mandates court review of detention. The United States and Afghanistan are parties to the ICCPR and must ensure that their actions comply with their treaty obligations. The Unlawful Enemy Combatant Review Board

(UECRB) procedures do not meet international legal standards governing detention and are an inadequate mechanism for challenging detention. Detainees are not provided notice of their allegations, not shown any evidence, not afforded counsel, and do not appear before an independent body to challenge their detention. These procedures do not comport with the requirement as articulated in human rights law. The International Committee of the Red Cross (ICRC) has also stated that detention in non-international armed conflict be pursuant to explicit law setting forth grounds and procedures.[154]

For future captures implement guidelines that minimize erroneous detention, loss of civilian life, and damage to property.

International military forces should work more closely with local communities and officials and with Afghan National Security Forces (ANSF)[155] to authenticate intelligence that is used to justify house raids and other hostilities in order to weed out faulty information based on personal and tribal animosities. International military forces should also develop guidance for conducting operations that demonstrates respect for religious and cultural values and minimizes damage to property during house searches and seizures.

For future captures implement reliable detainee documentation procedures.

In order to ensure that individuals are detained based on reliable information, soldiers and intelligence officers must be provided with proper training and support. Additional resources must be allocated to train soldiers and intelligence officers (including Afghan National Army soldiers who on certain operations work jointly with U.S. forces) in collection and maintenance of evidence to support detention, mitigate risks of erroneous detentions, and to facilitate future prosecution.

According to the Pentagon's May 2008 Detainee Operations, Joint Publication 3-63 guidelines, capturing units are supplied with flex-cuffs, goggles, zip-lock bags, trash bags, duct tape and evidence/property custody document forms. The military should assess, in consultation with JAGs, what additional supplies, such as cameras, markers, labels, rulers, etc. would be necessary to collect evidence at the point of capture.

■ Soldiers should be required to write a sworn statement describing the circumstances and reasons for the capture. This may involve basic training as to what information is relevant, including but not limited to the name of the detainee, the point of capture, evidence found with the detainee, witness names, and the reason for capture, including whether it was based on an intelligence source.

■ The intake officer at a Forward Operating Base (FOB), or any other detention facility, should be either a lawyer or, at minimum, a paralegal who should examine whether all evidence has been properly identified and whether the sworn statement is complete.

■ Intelligence officers who are involved in identifying a potential suspect for capture should be required to record the reasons in support of capture. Reasonable measures should be taken to protect the identity of informants. Efforts should be made to assess what information can be declassified so as to facilitate its use in prosecutions. This information should be included in the detainee's file as he is processed through the system.[156]

Continue releasing detainees and where there is evidence of criminal conduct transfer detainees for prosecution.

The United States military, which is capturing, interrogating and detaining individuals should continue releasing individuals and where there is evidence of criminal conduct under Afghan law should transfer the individual for criminal prosecution according to fair trial standards. (Individuals suspected of violating U.S. law should be lawfully transferred and prosecuted in U.S. courts.) Many acts, such as "assisting the enemy forces," destruction of government or private property, spying, conspiracy, sabotage, "propaganda against the government," treason, and engaging in "terror" activities, are prosecutable offenses under Afghan criminal law. Given the evidentiary concerns regarding trials in Afghan courts, the United States should:

■ Set up a legal task force to facilitate prosecutions of individuals it captures in Afghan courts.

● The United States military, which detained, interrogated, and imprisoned Bagram detainees and transfers them to Afghan custody, should take reasonable steps to support legitimate prosecutions in the Afghan courts. To strengthen judicial reform efforts in Afghanistan that the U.S. is presently engaged in and to facilitate prosecution of individuals it has detained, the United States should set up a legal task force in Afghanistan to support prosecutions as the U.S. military did in Iraq.

■ Apply lessons learned from Task Force 134 in Iraq.

● The U.S. military's Task Force 134 in Iraq has assisted with documentation of evidence and prosecution of insurgents in the Central Criminal Court of Iraq (CCCI). JAGs have trained soldiers and marines to collect evidence for criminal prosecution in Iraqi courts. U.S. soldiers have also appeared as witnesses in Iraqi courts, sometimes through video teleconference.[157] The Detainee Disposition Task Force should examine how Task Force 134 in Iraq assisted with evidence collection and criminal prosecutions in order to implement more effective rules and training for evidence collection in Afghanistan. Proper documentation of evidence and source information by intelligence officers and soldiers will lead to more reliable and fair prosecutions of detainees, reduce the risk of releasing dangerous detainees due to insufficient evidence, and minimize the risk of detaining innocents.

Grant human rights observers access to detainees and detention facilities in Afghanistan.

Afghan human rights organizations like the Afghan Independent Human Rights Commission (AIHRC) and international human rights organizations should be provided access to detainees and facilities where conflict-related detainees are held and should be allowed to meet with detainees privately so that a public, credible, and independent assessment can be made about conditions of confinement and interrogation techniques. Such access and reporting would set an example of transparency and inspire confidence that the U.S. is meeting its humane treatment obligations. The ICRC does not serve this function, as its findings are confidential.

Immediately cease bringing detainees to Afghanistan.

The United States acknowledges that some Bagram detainees were captured outside of Afghanistan. The British defense minister also has admitted that some individuals turned over to U.S. forces by the British military in Iraq were taken to Bagram.[158] The U.S. should stop rendering persons captured outside of Afghanistan to Bagram.

■ Repatriate or transfer detainees for prosecution.

- All persons captured outside Afghanistan and brought to Afghanistan must be repatriated to their country of origin for release or prosecution unless there is sufficient evidence to support criminal prosecution in U.S. courts. Upon repatriating detainees, the U.S. should turn over all evidence in its possession, including exculpatory evidence.

■ No transfers to torture.

- Undertake diplomatic efforts to resettle individuals for whom there are substantial grounds to believe that they will be at risk of torture if repatriated.

- The U.S. should stop rendering persons captured outside of Afghanistan to Bagram

VII. Appendices

A. Bagram Certificate for Release

DEPARTMENT OF DEFENSE
COMBINED/JOINT TASK FORCE (CJTF)-101
BAGRAM AIRFIELD, AFGHANISTAN
APO AE 09354

CJTF-101-JA-DETOPS   6 March 2009

MEMORANDUM FOR RECORD

SUBJECT: Certificate for Release of ███████████████, ████████████

1. This memorandum is to certify that the following individual was detained by the
United States Armed Forces from 20 November 2007 to 6 March 2009.

Official ISN	First Name	Last Name	DOB	Country of Birth	Son of
US9AF-██████	██████████	████████	1 JAN 79	AFGHANISTAN	████████████

2. This individual has been determined to pose no threat to the United States Armed
Forces or its interests in Afghanistan. There are no charges from the United States
pending against this individual at this time. The United States government intends that
this person be fully rejoined with his family. This certificate has no bearing on future
misconduct.

CJTF-101 Det Ops, JA, NCOIC

General Powers of Notary Public
Judge Advocate United States Army
10 U.S.C. 1044

B. Certificate of Appreciation of Former Bagram Prisoner

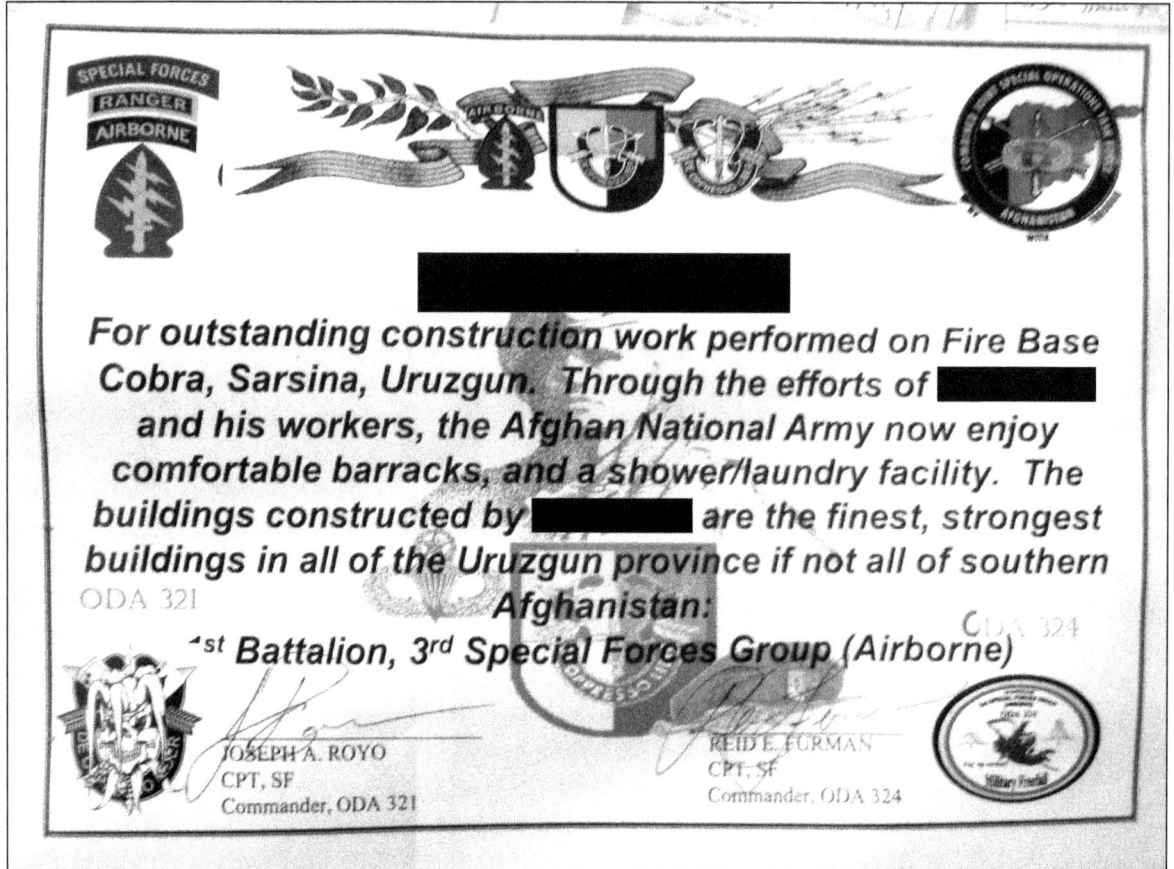

For outstanding construction work performed on Fire Base Cobra, Sarsina, Uruzgun. Through the efforts of ▮▮▮ and his workers, the Afghan National Army now enjoy comfortable barracks, and a shower/laundry facility. The buildings constructed by ▮▮▮ are the finest, strongest buildings in all of the Uruzgun province if not all of southern Afghanistan:

ODA 321

ODA 324

1st Battalion, 3rd Special Forces Group (Airborne)

JOSEPH A. ROYO
CPT, SF
Commander, ODA 321

REID E. FURMAN
CPT, SF
Commander, ODA 324

VIII. Endnotes

[1] *See generally*, Seth G. Jones, *The Rise of Afghanistan's Insurgency: State Failure and Jihad*, 32 Int'l Security 4 (2008).

[2] ABC News/BBC/ARD Poll, "Support for U.S. Efforts Plummets Amid Afghanistan's Ongoing Strife," February 9, 2009, http://abcnews.go.com/images/PollingUnit/1083a1Afghanistan2009.pdf.

[3] Executive Order No. 13,493, *Review of Detention Policy Options* (January 22, 2009).

[4] Human Rights First telephone interview with U.S. CENTCOM (name withheld), May 14, 2009.

[5] Kenneth Katzman, *Afghanistan: Post-Taliban Governance, Security, and U.S. Policy*, Congressional Research Service, RL30588, February 9, 2009.

[6] *Bakri v. Bush*, No. 1:08-1307, Declaration of Colonel Charles A. Tennison, dated September 15, 2008, submitted in support of Respondents' Motion to Dismiss ("Tennison Declaration"), ¶6.

[7] Ibid.

[8] Ibid., ¶9.

[9] U.S. Department of Defense, Combined Forces Command-Afghanistan Area of Operations (CFC-A AO) Detainee Operations, Report of Inspection, June 26, 2004, p. 20 (also known as the "Jacoby Report").

[10] Ibid.

[11] U.S. Embassy, Kabul, Afghanistan, "Detainee Transfers to Afghanistan," press release, August 4, 2005, http://kabul.usembassy.gov/pr080405.html.

[12] Tim Golden, "Foiling US Plans, Prison Expands in Afghanistan, *New York Times*, January 18, 2008.

[13] Ibid.

[14] U.S. President George W. Bush and Afghan President Hamid Karzai, "Joint Declaration of the United States-Afghanistan Strategic Partnership," White House Press Release, May 23, 2005.

[15] Ibid.; *see also* Kenneth Katzman, *Afghanistan: Post-War Governance, Security, and U.S. Policy*, Congressional Research Service Report for Congress, RL30588, January 28, 2008.

[16] Testimony of Secretary of Defense Robert M. Gates, Senate Committee on the Armed Services, 111th Cong., 1st sess., January 27, 2009.

[17] *See, e.g.*, James Kirkup, "Britain Accused of Complicity in U.S. 'rendition' programme," *Telegraph (Chatham)*, February 26, 2009 (British Defense Secretary John Hutton told the British parliament that two Pakistani men held by British forces in Iraq were handed over to the Americans in 2004 and transported out of the country and still being held in Afghanistan).

[18] Christopher Weaver, "Pentagon Keeps Mum on Who's in Bagram," *ProPublica*, January 28, 2009.

[19] International Committee of the Red Cross, "U.S. detention related to the fight against terrorism—the role of the ICRC," April 3, 2009, http://www.icrc.org/web/eng/siteeng0.nsf/html/united-states-detention-faq-240209.

[20] Eric Schmitt and Tim Golden, "U.S. Planning Big New Prison in Afghanistan," *New York Times*, May 17, 2008.

[21] Tennison Declaration, *supra* note 6, ¶9.

[22] U.S. Department of Defense, The Department of Defense Detainee Program, Directive 2310.01E (September 5, 2006), p. 9.

[23] Ibid., p. 33.

[24] Detainee Review Board Procedures at Bagram Theater Internment Facility (BTIF). Afghanistan, attached as an appendix to Brief of Respondent-Appellants appeal to the U.S. Court of Appeals for the District of Columbia, Al Maqalah v. Gates, Nos. 09-5265, 09-5266, 09-5277 (D.C. Cir. September 14, 2009) ("2009 DRB Procedures").

[25] According to a November 2006 affidavit of Col. Rose Miller, Commander of Detention Operations in Bagram, the review board was called "Enemy Combatant Review Board" (ECRB) and consisted of five commissioned officers who evaluated a detainee's status. The change to UECRB occurred sometime in 2007 and now comprises of three officers rather than five. *Ruzatullah v. Rumsfeld*, No. 07-CV-07107 (D.D.C. November 19, 2006).

[26] Tennison Declaration, *supra* note 6, ¶13.

[27] Ibid. ¶13.

[28] Ibid.

[29] Ibid.

[30] Ibid.

[31] Ibid.

[32] Human Rights First telephone conversation with CENTCOM official (name withheld), May 14, 2009.

[33] Ibid.

[34] S.C. Res. 1386, U.N. Doc. S/RES/1386 (December 20, 2001).

[35] ISAF's authority was expanded to cover the whole of Afghanistan in 2003. S.C. Res. 1510, U.N. Doc. S/RES/1510 (October 13, 2003). Additional Security Council Resolutions relating to ISAF include: S.C. Res. 1413, U.N. Doc. S/RES/1413 (May 23, 2002); S.C. Res. 1444, U.N. Doc. S/RES/1444 (November 27, 2002); S.C. Res. 1563, U.N. Doc. S/RES/1563 (December 17, 2004); S.C. Res. 1623, U.N. Doc. S/RES/1623 (September 13, 2005); S.C. Res. 1707, U.N. Doc. S/RES/1707 (September 12, 2006); S.C. Res. 1776, U.N. Doc. S/RES/1776 (September 19, 2007); S.C. Res. 1833, U.N. Doc. S/RES/1833 (September 22, 2008).

[36] Ashley Deeks, *Detention in Afghanistan: The Need for an Integrated Plan*, Center for Strategic and International Studies (February 14, 2008).

[37] Draft Technical Agreement Between the Government of the Islamic Republic of Afghanistan and the North Atlantic Treaty Organization as a Framework to Improve Methods and Procedures for the Prosecution of the Global War on Terrorism to Ensure our Joint Success (January 2009), on file with Human Rights First ("Draft Technical Agreement").

[38] Jason Straziuso and Amir Shah, "Afghanistan Seeks Control Over NATO Deployments," *Associated Press*, January 20, 2009.

[39] *Draft Technical Agreement*, *supra* note 37.

[40] Human Rights First interview with Lt. Col. Steven Weir, Deputy Staff Judge Advocate, U.S. Forces-Afghanistan, Kabul, Afghanistan, April 26, 2009.

[41] Ibid.

[42] Ibid.

[43] International Committee of the Red Cross, "U.S. detention related to the events of 11 September 2001 and its aftermath—the role of the ICRC," July 30, 2008, http://www.icrc.org/web/eng/siteeng0.nsf/htmlall/usa-detention-update-121205?opendocument ("ICRC U.S. Detention Related to 9/11").

[44] *Maqaleh v. Gates*, Memorandum Opinion, No. 06-1669, (D.D.C. April 2, 2009).

[45] For a detailed study on night raids *see* Afghan Independent Human Rights Commission, *From Hope to Fear: An Afghan Perspective on Operations of Pro-Government Forces in Afghanistan* (December 2008).

[46] Human Rights First interview with N.K., Kabul, Afghanistan, April 19, 2009.

[47] Afghans living near the Pakistan border use rupees, as well as Afghanis and U.S. dollars as currency.

[48] Human Rights First interview with M.A., Jalalabad, Afghanistan, April 23, 2009.

[49] Human Rights First interview with A.M., Jalalabad, Afghanistan, April 23, 2009.

[50] Human Rights First interview with M.K., Jalalabad, Afghanistan, April 24, 2009.

[51] Kim Barker, "Death of Afghan Elder Raises Tension," *Chicago Tribune*, June 26, 2005.

[52] Ibid.

[53] Ibid.

[54] Human Rights First interview with K. A., Jalalabad, Afghanistan, April 23, 2009.

[55] Human Rights First interview with B.Z., Kabul, Afghanistan, April 28, 2009.

[56] Ibid.

[57] Ibid.

[58] Human Rights First interview with M.I., Jalalabad, Afghanistan, April 24, 2009.

[59] Human Rights First interview with J.G., Jalalabad, Afghanistan, April 24, 2009.

[60] Human Rights First interview with S.M., Jalalabad, Afghanistan, April 23, 2009.

[61] Ibid.

[62] U.S. Department of Defense, Directive 2310.01E, *supra* note 22.

[63] Human Rights First interview with M.A., Jalalabad, Afghanistan, April 23, 2009.

[64] Human Rights First interview with K.H., Jalalabad, Afghanistan, April 23, 2009.

[65] Human Rights First interview with M.N., Jalalabad, Afghanistan, April 24, 2009.

[66] Human Rights First interview with members of the ANDF review committee (names withheld), Kabul, Afghanistan, April 20, 2009.

[67] Human Rights First interview with B.Z. (name withheld), Kabul, Afghanistan, April 28, 2009.

[68] Human Rights First interview with J.G., Jalalabad, Afghanistan, April 24, 2009.

[69] Human Rights First interview with M.A., Jalalabad, Afghanistan, April 24, 2009.

[70] Richard Oppell, "U.S. Captain Hears Pleas for Afghan Detainee," *New York Times*, May 24, 2009.

[71] Ibid.

[72] David Kilcullen, *The Accidental Guerrilla: Fighting Small Wars in the Midst of a Big One* (New York: Oxford University Press, 2009), pp. 39-41, 85-86, 96; "For Pakistan's Pashtuns, Tribe Outweighs Nationality," *St. Petersburg Times*, October 28, 2001.

[73] Human Rights First interview with LTC Steven Weir, Deputy Staff Judge Advocate, U.S. Forces- Afghanistan, ISAF Compound, Kabul, Afghanistan, April 26, 2009.

[74] Ibid.

[75] Ibid.

[76] Human Rights First interview with B.Z., Kabul, Afghanistan, April 28, 2009.

[77] *Maqaleh*, Memorandum Opinion, *supra* note 44.

[78] ICRC U.S. Detention Related to 9/11, *supra* note 43 .

[79] Carlotta Gall, "U.S. Military Investigating Death of Afghan in Custody," *New York Times*, March 4, 2003; Tim Golden, "In U.S. Report, Brutal Details of 2 Afghan Inmates' Deaths," *New York Times*, May 20, 2005; Dana Priest and Barton Gellman, "U.S. Decries Abuse but Defends Interrogations," *Washington Post*, December 26, 2002; "U.S. general: Details in probe of Afghan jails to stay secret," *Associated Press*, June 1, 2004.

[80] Human Rights First interview with G.K., Kabul, Afghanistan, April 22, 2009.

[81] Human Rights First interview with A.B., Kabul, Afghanistan, April 22, 2009.

[82] Ibid.

[83] *Maqaleh*, Memorandum Opinion, *supra* note 44.

[84] *Maqaleh v. Gates*, No. 1:06-699, Declaration of Colonel Joe E. Etheridge, dated January 15, 2009, submitted in support of Respondents' Response to This Court's Order of January 7, 2009 (D.D.C. January 16, 2009) ("Etheridge Declaration").

[85] *Maqaleh*, Memorandum Opinion, *supra* note 44.

[86] *Maqaleh v. Gates*, No. 06-1669, Motion for Certification of this Court's April 2, 2009 Order for Interlocutory Appeal Pursuant to 28 U.S.C. § 1292(b) and for a Stay of Proceedings Pending Appeal (D.D.C. April 10, 2009) and *Maqaleh v. Gates*, No. 06-1669, Memorandum Opinion and Order (D.D.C. June 1, 2009) (granting stay).

[87] *Wazir v. Gates*, No. 06-1697, Memorandum Order (D.D.C. June 26, 2009).

[88] *Maqaleh*, Memorandum Opinion, *supra* note 44, at 37.

[89] Ibid.

[90] Human Rights First interview with N.K., Kabul, Afghanistan, April 19, 2009.

[91] Human Rights First interview with M.I., Jalalabad, Afghanistan, April 24, 2009.

[92] Human Rights First interview with M.K., Jalalabad, Afghanistan, April 24, 2009.

[93] Human Rights First interview with N.K., Kabul, Afghanistan, April 19, 2009.

[94] Human Rights First interview with G.K., Kabul, Afghanistan, April 22, 2009.

[95] Human Rights First interview with G.K, A.B., and A.K., Kabul, Afghanistan, April 22, 2009.

[96] Human Rights First interview with A.B., Kabul, Afghanistan, April 22, 2009.

[97] Human Rights First interview with G.K., Kabul, Afghanistan, April 22, 2009.

[98] Carlotta Gall, "Video Link Plucks Afghan Detainees From Black Hole of Isolation," *New York Times*, April 13, 2008.

[99] International Committee of the Red Cross, "Afghanistan: Family Visit Programme Begins for Bagram Detainees," September 23, 2008, http://www.icrc.org/Web/eng/siteeng0.nsf/html/afghanistan-feature-230908.

[100] Golden, "Foiling US Plans, Prison Expands in Afghanistan," *supra* note 12.

[101] *See also Ex Detainees Allege Bagram Abuse*, BBC News, June 24, 2009, available at http://news.bbc.co.uk/2/hi/south_asia/8116046.stm (the BBC interviewed 27 former Bagram detainees who alleged that they were subjected to stress positions, sleep deprivation, threatened with dogs, excessive heat or cold, loud noise, and forced to remove clothes in front of female soldiers).

[102] Human Rights First interview with J.G., Jalalabad, Afghanistan, April 24, 2009.

[103] Human Rights First interview with I.M., Jalalabad, Afghanistan, April 24, 2009.

[104] For a detailed study on compensation payments by NATO, including the United States, *see* Campaign for Innocent Victims In Conflict, *Losing the People: The Costs and Consequences of Civilian Suffering in Afghanistan*, January 2009.

[105] The flaws in the ANDF trials, as detailed in *Arbitrary Justice*, violate article 14 of the ICCPR which provides a defendant the right to confront evidence against oneself. This right requires that an accused should be given "adequate and proper opportunity to challenge and question a witness against him, either at the time the witness was making his statement or at some later stage of the proceedings." A conviction thus cannot be substantially based on the statements of witnesses whom the defense counsel is unable to cross-examine. *See* European Court of Human Rights, *Kostovski v. The Netherlands* (App. 11454/85), Judgment of 20 November 1989; (1990) 12 EHRR 434; David J. Harris, Michael O'Boyle and C. Warbrick, *Law of the European Convention on Human Rights* (London: Butterworths) (1995), p. 212.

[106] 2004 Interim Criminal Procedure Code for Courts, arts. 23, 38, 51, 53 (ICPC). The ICPC is being revised.

[107] Ibid., arts. 37-38, 43, 55.

[108] Human Rights First interview with member of the ANDF review committee (name withheld), Kabul, Afghanistan, April 20, 2009.

[109] Ibid.

[110] Ibid.

[111] Ibid.

[112] Human Rights First interview with national security prosecutor (name withheld), Kabul, Afghanistan, April 26, 2009.

[113] Ibid.

[114] Human Rights First interview with Mohammad Ishaq Aloko, Kabul, Afghanistan, April 25, 2009.

[115] Ibid.

[116] Center for Policy and Development, *Bridging Modernity and Tradition: Rule of Law*, Afghanistan Human Development Report 2007, p.8.

[117] *See generally*, United Nations Assistance Mission in Afghanistan, *Arbitrary Detention in Afghanistan: A Call for Action*, vol. 1, *Overview and Recommendations*, January 2009; United Nations Assistance Mission in Afghanistan, *Arbitrary Detention in Afghanistan: A Call for Action*, vol.2, *A Practical Guide to Understanding and Combating Arbitrary Detention Practices in Afghanistan*, January 2009 (concluding that "Afghanistan's legal and regulatory frameworks are inadequate and do not include critical rights or guidance to authorities. Afghanistan's formal justice system is still developing

institutions, knowledge, capacity and tools and creates systematic weaknesses that allow arbitrary detentions. Impunity, corruption and weak oversight mechanisms enable arbitrary detention practices to continue uncorrected. Training and capacity-building programmes are insufficient to tackle the conceptual gaps between most Afghans' understanding of justice and the concepts contained in the formal justice system").

[118] U.N. Economic and Social Council, Commission on Human Rights, Sixty-Second Session, *Report of the High Commissioner for Human Rights on the Situation of Human Rights in Afghanistan and on the Achievements of Technical Assistance in the Field of Human Rights*, U.N. Doc. E/CN.4/2006/108 (March 3, 2006).

[119] In November 2007, Louise Arbour, the United Nations High Commissioner for Human Rights, visited Afghanistan and noted her concern: "Transfers to the [NDS] are particularly problematic, given that it is not a regular law enforcement body and operates on the basis of a secret decree. I urged the President to ensure greater transparency, access to, and accountability for this institution, starting with publication of the decree on which its powers are based." United Nations Office at Geneva, "High Commissioner for Human Rights Concludes Visit to Afghanistan," press release, November 20, 2007.

[120] *See* Anthony H. Cordesman, Adam Mausner, and David Kasten, *Winning in Afghanistan: Creating Effective Afghan Security Forces*, Center for Strategic & International Studies, May 2009. The U.S. is involved in rule of issues primarily through five agencies: the Department of Defense (DOD), the Department of State's Bureau for International Narcotics and Law Enforcement Affairs (INL), the U.S. Agency for International Development (USAID), the Department of Justice (DOJ) and the Drug Enforcement Agency. DOD coordinates military justice reform through the Combined Security Transition Command-Afghanistan (CTSC-A).

[121] S.C. Res. 1833, U.N. Doc. S/RES/1833 (September 22, 2008).

[122] A Supreme Court decree issued in 2008, on file with Human Rights First, mandates automatic review by the Afghan Supreme Court of an acquittal of a defendant charged under the Internal and External Security Act or for narcotics smuggling.

[123] Human Rights First interview with national security prosecutor (name withheld), Kabul, Afghanistan, April 26, 2009.

[124] Sam Yousufazai and Ron Moreau, "Afghan Prison Blues," *Newsweek*, February 11, 2008 (describing how Taliban members bribed their way out of NDS custody); Sami Yousafzai, "Inside the Prison Escape," *Newsweek*, June 30, 2008 (describing how Taliban fighters and other prisoners broke out of Sarposa prison in Kandahar which had 15-20 men crammed in tiny cells and allowed inmates to pay $100 a month to possess mobile phones); Hamid Shalizi, "Knives, Petrol Bombs Found in Afghan Prisons," *Reuters*, July 5, 2008. (describing how Afghan security forces found knives, petrol bombs, and mobile phones in Pul-e-Charkhi prison outside of Kabul).

[125] Human Rights First telephone interview with U.S. CENTCOM official (name withheld), May 14, 2009.

[126] Human Rights First interview with national security prosecutor (name withheld), Kabul, Afghanistan, April 26, 2009.

[127] *See* Major W. James Annexstad, "The Detention and Prosecution of Insurgents and Other Non-Traditional Combatants—A Look at the Task Force 134 Process and Future of Detainee Prosecutions," *Army Lawyer*, July 2007. Human Rights First has not examined the trials at CCCI and cannot attest to the fairness of the proceedings. Nor have we examined the adequacy of the investigations to build a criminal case by Task Force 134. The comparison to Task Force 134 is to show that the U.S. military has engaged in evidence gathering and makes soldiers available for testimony in Iraqi criminal trials of persons captured by the U.S.

[128] The term "international armed conflict" does not mean armed conflict that is "transnational." It is one of two varieties of armed conflict and is referred to in Common Article 2 of the Geneva Conventions as "armed conflict which may arise between two or more of the High Contracting Parties. . . ." All other armed conflict, be it internal or transnational, is non-international. The terms international and non-international are understood to refer to the identity of the parties to the armed conflict, not to the scope of territory in which the conflict is being fought. Thus, hostilities between a state and an armed group are governed by Common Article 3, so long as they occur on the territory of one of the parties to the Conventions. It is perfectly feasible to have international armed conflict confined to the borders of one State and non-international armed conflict either spill over the borders of one State to another. This understanding of the term "non-international armed conflict" was confirmed by the U. S. Supreme Court in *Hamdan v. Rumsfeld*, 548 U.S. 557 (2006). The majority opinion of Justice Stevens rejected the position of the government that Common Article 3 does not apply to the armed conflict with al Qaeda because that conflict is "international in scope."

[129] The Bush Administration failed to recognize the applicability of the Geneva Conventions when it launched the armed conflict in Afghanistan. In a memorandum dated February 7, 2002, President George W. Bush determined that:

- the President has the authority to "suspend Geneva" but declined to do so;
- "the provisions of Geneva will apply to our present conflict with the Taliban," but that Taliban fighters are "unlawful combatants" who do not qualify as prisoners of war under the Third Geneva Convention;
- the Geneva Conventions are inapplicable to al Qaeda because it is not a state party to the Conventions; and

■ "Common Article 3 of Geneva does not apply to either al Qaeda or Taliban detainees, because, among other reasons, the relevant conflicts are international in scope and common Article 3 applies only to 'armed conflict not of an international character.'"

With the exception of the conclusion that the Geneva Conventions did apply to the conflict with the Taliban, each one of these assertions is unsupported by law. In addition, the February 2002 memo did not mention applicability of the Fourth Geneva Convention to Taliban members denied PoW status, al Qaeda members presumptively qualified for civilian status, and others who were alleged to be neither Taliban nor al Qaeda. In other words, the February 2002 memo conceded the application of the Geneva Conventions to the conflict with the Taliban, but without affording any of the protections contained therein. Going forward, it is essential for U.S. policy-makers to reverse these mistakes in order to provide a legal basis for U.S. detention in Afghanistan.

[130] *See* Legality of the Threat or Use of Nuclear Weapons, Advisory Opinion, 1996 I.C.J. 226, ¶ 25 (July 8); Legal Consequences of the Construction of a Wall in the Occupied Palestinian Territory, Advisory Opinion, 2004 I.C.J. 136, ¶ 106 (July 9); Armed Activities on the Territory of the Congo (New Application 2002), (Democratic Republic of Congo v. Rwanda), 2006 I.C.J. ¶ 119; U.N. Human Rights Committee, General Comment No. 31 [80] Nature of the General Legal Obligation Imposed on States Parties to the Covenant, ¶ 11, U.N. Doc. CCPR/C/21/Rev.1/Add.13, (May 26, 2005). Numerous Security Council and General Assembly resolutions affirming the principle that human rights law remains applicable during armed conflict. *See, e.g.,* S.C. Res. 1674, U.N. Doc. S/RES/1674 (April 28, 2006); S.C. Res. 1502, U.N. Doc. S/RES/1502 (August 26, 2003); S.C. Res. 1355, ¶ 15, 35, U.N. Doc. S/RES/1355 (June 15, 2001); S.C. Res. 1296, ¶ 5, U.N. Doc. S/RES/1296 (April 19, 2000); S.C. Res. 237, U.N. Doc. S/RES/237 (June 14, 1967); G.A. Res. 2444(XXIII), (1978), U.N. Doc GA/RES/2444 (December 19, 1968); Report of the International Commission of Inquiry on Darfur to the U.N. Secretary-General (January 25, 2005) (Pursuant to S.C. Res. 1564 (September 18, 2004)). For analysis of the interaction between IHL and IHRL in relation to detention *see* Jean-Marie Henckaerts and Louise Doswald-Beck, *Customary International Humanitarian Law*, International Committee of the Red Cross (Cambridge Univ. Press, 2005), vol. 1, pp. 299-494.

[131] According to the Bonn Agreement, art. 1: "An Interim Authority shall be established upon the official transfer of power on 22 December 2001. . . ." Art. 3: "Upon the official transfer of power, the Interim Authority shall be the repository of Afghan sovereignty, with immediate effect." *See Agreement on Provisional Arrangements in Afghanistan Pending the Re-Establishment of Permanent Government Institutions* (December 5, 2001).

[132] Although neither the United States nor Afghanistan is a party to AP II, much of its content is widely deemed to be customary international humanitarian law. *See also* Henckaerts, *Customary International Humanitarian Law, supra* note 130 (the ICRC's authoritative iteration of customary IHL).

[133] International Committee of the Red Cross, "International humanitarian law and terrorism: questions and answers," May 5, 2004, http://coe-dmha.org/TAPpdfs/IIIMEF2006/Resource%20Materials/International%20Law/IHL%20docs/Handbooks,%20Guidance%20references/IHL%20&%20Terrorism.pdf.

[134] *See* Geneva Convention (III) Relative to the Treatment of Prisoners of War, Aug. 12, 1949, 75 U.N.T.S. 135, art. 21 and Geneva Convention (IV) Relative to the Protection of Civilian Persons in Time of War, Aug. 12, 1949, 75 U.N.T.S. 287, art. 42.

[135] The term "combatant" as understood in the laws of war is limited to members of armed forces of a state or to others who possess a "privilege of belligerency." Because non-state fighters possess no privilege of belligerency and because they cannot qualify for PoW status even in an international armed conflict, they are not considered "combatants." They remain civilians who directly participate in hostilities, and for that reason, may be targeted under the laws of war, as well as detained under domestic law.

[136] There are no "combatants" in non-international armed conflict, as that term is understood in IHL, other than the armed forces of the state. Former ICRC head of legal division Marco Sassòli has opined that: "In such (non-international) conflicts, IHL cannot possibly be seen as providing a sufficient legal basis for detaining anyone. It simply provides for guarantees of humane treatment and, in prosecutions for criminal offenses, for certain judicial guarantees of independence and impartiality. Possible bases for arrest, detention or internment are entirely governed by domestic legislation and the human rights law requirement that no one be deprived of his or her liberty except on such grounds and in accordance with procedures as are established by law. In State practice too, governments confronted by non-international armed conflicts base arrests, detentions, and internment of rebels, including rebel fighters, either on domestic criminal law or on special security legislation introduced during the conflict. They never invoke the 'law of war.'" Marco Sassòli, "Query: Is There a Status of 'Unlawful Combatant'?" in *International Law Studies, Issues in International Law and Military Operations*, ed. Richard B. Jaques (Newport: Naval War College, 2006) 80:64.

[137] International Committee of the Red Cross, *International Humanitarian Law and the Challenges of Contemporary Armed Conflicts*, 30th International Conference of the Red Cross and Red Crescent (Geneva: November 2007), p. 11 ("2007 ICRC IHL Conference") and Jelena Pejic, *Procedural Principles and Safeguards for Internment/Administrative Detention in Armed Conflict and Other Situations of Violence*, 87 International Review of the Red Cross 375 (2005).

[138] Authorization for Use of Military Force, Pub. L. No. 107-40, 115 Stat. 224 (2001). *See also Hamdan*, 548 U.S. at 630 ("The Court of Appeals thought, and the Government asserts, that Common Article 3 does not apply to Hamdan because the conflict with al Qaeda, being 'international in scope,' does not qualify as a 'conflict not of an international character.' [internal citations omitted]. That reasoning is erroneous. The term 'conflict not of an international character' is used here in contradistinction to a conflict between nations.")

[139] In 2004, a plurality of the Supreme Court in *Hamdi v. Rumsfeld* held that the AUMF authorized detention of an individual, Hamdi, captured during what was then an international armed conflict between the United States and Afghanistan. The Supreme Court rested its decision in *Hamdi* on the principle that "[t]he capture and detention of lawful combatants and the capture, detention, and trial of unlawful combatants, by universal agreement and practice, are important incident[s] of war." 52 U.S. 507, 518 (2004) (internal quotation marks and citation omitted); see also ibid. at 519 ("[D]etention to prevent a combatant's return to the battlefield is a fundamental incident of waging war . . . ."). The Court's decision thus justifies detention of "combatants" only—a term the Court does not define. As discussed in notes 158-59, while the term "combatant" has an established meaning in the law of international armed conflict, the term is technically inapposite in the NIAC context. The term "combatant," as used in IHL, applies to those who have a legal privilege to directly participate in hostilities—i.e., members of a state's regular armed forces and militias. All others, including those who support the armed forces (such as military suppliers and contractors) and those who take up arms in the conflict absent a privilege to do so under IHL and in violation of domestic criminal law, are considered civilians. In a NIAC, non-state fighters have no legal right under domestic law to take up arms or to enjoy immunity for their acts of war even though their participation in hostilities is not a violation of IHL so long as they target military objectives with legitimate means. Accordingly, none are considered "combatants."

[140] AUMF, *supra* note 138.

[141] Pejic, *Procedural Principles and Safeguards for Internment/Administrative Detention*, *supra* note 137.

[142] International Committee of the Red Cross, "International humanitarian law and terrorism: questions and answers," May 5, 2004, http://coe-dmha.org/TAPpdfs/IIIMEF2006/Resource%20Materials/International%20Law/IHL%20docs/Handbooks,%20Guidance%20references/IHL%20&%20Terrorism.pdf.

[143] 2007 ICRC IHL Conference, p. 11, *supra* note 137.

[144] Article 9(1) of the ICCPR provides: "everyone has the right to liberty and security of persons. No one shall be subjected to arbitrary arrest and detention. No one shall be deprived of his liberty except on such grounds and in accordance with such procedure as are established by law." The drafting history of article 9(1) "confirms that 'arbitrariness' is not to be equated with 'against the law,' but must be interpreted more broadly to include elements of inappropriateness, injustice and lack of predictability." Thus, deprivation of liberty, even though it may be authorized by positive domestic law, should not be "manifestly unproportional, unjust or unpredictable, and that the specific manner in which an arrest is made must not be discriminatory and must be able to be deemed appropriate and proportional in view of the circumstances of the case." Manfred Nowak, *U.N. Covenant on Civil and Political Rights: CCPR Commentary* (Kehl am Rhein: N.P. Engel, 1993) pp. 172-173.

[145] The United Nations Human Rights Committee, the authoritative body which interprets the ICCPR and monitors state compliance with the treaty, has interpreted Art. 9(4) to require "[d]ue process, independence of the reviewing courts from the executive branch and the army, access of detainees to counsel of their choice and to all proceedings and evidence." Office of the U.N. High Commissioner for Human Rights, Human Rights Committee, *Concluding observations of the Human Rights Committee: United States of America*, U.N. Doc. CCPR/C/USA/CO/3/Rev.1, at ¶ 18 (December 18, 2006).

[146] ICCPR, art. 4(1). The ICCPR instructs that such measures must be necessary, must be limited "to the extent strictly required by the exigencies of the situation," and must not be inconsistent with the State's other obligations under international law. Derogation must also not be applied discriminatorily.

[147] The ICCPR also prohibits derogation from the right not to be held in slavery, the right not to be imprisoned for the inability to fulfill a contractual obligation, prohibition against ex post facto application of the law, right to recognition as a person before the law, and the right to freedom of thought, conscience, and religion (arts. 8, 11, 15, 16, 18 respectively).

[148] U.N. Human Rights Committee, General Comment No. 29 States of Emergency (Article 4), U.N. Doc. CCPR/C/21/Rev.1/Add.11, August 31, 2001, para. 6 (General Comment No. 29) ("In order to protect non-derogable rights, the right to take proceedings before a court to enable the court to decide without delay on the lawfulness of detention, must not be diminished by a State party's decision to derogate from the Covenant.")

[149] 2007 ICRC IHL Conference, *supra* note 138, p. 11 referring to Annex 1: Pejic, *Procedural Principles and Safeguards*.

[150] Pejic, *Procedural Principles and Safeguards*, *supra* note 137, pp. 384-390.

[151] Ibid.

[152] Secretary of Defense Robert M. Gates, Speech, National Defense University, Washington, D.C., September 29, 2008; "Seven Questions: Gen. David Petraeus on Winding down the Surge," Foreign Policy, January 2008.

[153] The 2007 *Rule of Law Handbook: A Practitioner's Guide for Judge Advocates* states that: "In light of the need to establish the legitimacy of the rule of law among the host nation's populace, conduct by US forces that would be questionable under any mainstream interpretation of international human rights law is unlikely to have a place in rule of law operations." *Rule of Law Handbook: A Practitioner's Guide for Judge Advocates*, Center for Law and Military Operations, The Judge Advocate General's Legal Center and School, U.S. Army, and Joint Force Judge Advocate, U,S. Joint Forces Command, July 2007, p. 67.

[154] Pejic, *Procedural Principles and Safeguards*, *supra* note 137.

[155] ANSF includes Afghan National Army (ANA), Afghan National Police (ANP), and Afghan National Army Air Corps (ANAAC).

[156] These recommendations are based on conversations with former JAG officers who served in Iraq.

[157] See Major W. James Annexstad, "The Detention and Prosecution of Insurgents and Other Non-Traditional Combatants—A Look at the Task Force 134 Process and Future of Detainee Prosecutions," Army Lawyer, July 2007. Human Rights First has not examined the trials at CCCI and cannot attest to the fairness of the proceedings. Nor have we examined the adequacy of the investigations to build a criminal case by Task Force 134. The comparison to Task Force 134 is to show that the U.S. military has been engaged in evidence gathering and has made soldiers available for testimony in Iraqi criminal trials of persons captured by the U.S.

[158] See, e.g., James Kirkup, "Britain Accused of Complicity in U.S. 'rendition' programme," Telegraph (Chatham), February 26, 2009 (British Defense Secretary John Hutton told the British parliament that two Pakistani men held by British forces in Iraq were handed over to the Americans in 2004 and transported out of the country and are still being held in Afghanistan). In habeas proceedings before Judge Bates, petitioners who are nationals of Yemen, Tunisia, and Afghanistan were reportedly taken into custody in Pakistan, Thailand, and United Arab Emirates and then transferred to Bagram. See generally, Maqaleh, Memorandum Opinion, *supra* note 44.

Fixing Bagram

Strengthening Detention Reforms to Align with U.S. Strategic Priorities

November 2009

Table of Contents

Fixing Bagram

Strengthening Detention Reforms to Align with U.S. Strategic Priorities

I. Overview

Eight years after launching Operation Enduring Freedom (OEF) in Afghanistan—with a mission to kill and capture "high-value" al Qaeda and Taliban members and destroy the safe havens from which al Qaeda planned and directed the 9/11 attacks—the United States government has announced several significant detention reforms in Afghanistan. Human Rights First has closely monitored U.S. detention policies and practices since September 11, 2001. In this paper, we analyze the new detention reforms announced in September 2009 and make recommendations for further improvement in U.S. detention practices in line with U.S. policy interests and legal obligations. We base our recommendations on an analysis of the applicable humanitarian and human rights law and field visits to Afghanistan.

In September 2009, the Pentagon announced improved detainee review board (DRB) procedures for detainees being held by the U.S. military at the Bagram Theater Internment Facility (BTIF) at Bagram Air Base, Afghanistan. The Pentagon also announced reforms to both U.S. and Afghan prisons focused on rehabilitation and skills training of prisoners in order to prevent radicalization, as well as an assessment on evidentiary gaps that hinder

successful and fair prosecution of suspected insurgents transferred by international military forces to Afghan courts. These reforms reflect an understanding on the part of the Obama administration that the role of detention must be carefully calibrated to provide optimal protection to U.S. troops and to the Afghan population, while at the same time, minimizing the risk of alienating the very population U.S. troops are there to protect. Time will tell whether these reforms will be implemented effectively and can resolve the underlying problems of arbitrary and indefinite detention, mistaken captures, and lack of evidence for legitimate prosecutions in Afghan courts.

General Stanley McChrystal, Commander of U.S. Forces-Afghanistan (U.S.FOR-A) and the International Security Assistance Forces (ISAF), in his August 2009 assessment on Afghanistan stated that:

> Detention operations, while critical to successful counterinsurgency operations, also have the potential to become a strategic liability for the U.S. and ISAF. With the drawdown in Iraq and the closing of Guantanamo Bay, the focus on U.S. detention operations will turn to the U.S. Bagram Theater Internment Facility (BTIF). Because of the classification level of the BTIF and the lack

of public transparency, the Afghan people see U.S. detention operations as secretive and lacking in due process. It is critical that we continue to develop and build capacity to empower the Afghan government to conduct all detentions operations in this country in accordance with international and national law. [1]

The detention reforms initiated by the Obama administration appear to fit within the "integrated civilian-military counterinsurgency strategy in Afghanistan" announced by President Obama on March 27, 2009 to "integrate population security with building effective local governance and economic development" and "establish the security needed to provide space and time for stabilization and reconstruction activities."[2]

The emphasis on security for the Afghan population is essential to build and maintain support for American military presence and to marginalize support for insurgents. A 2009 ABC News poll found that only 37 percent of Afghans say they support Western forces, down from 67 percent in 2006.[3] The poll data is consistent with the conversations Human Rights First had with former prisoners detained by the U.S. military in Afghanistan at Bagram Air Base, Afghan civilians, and government officials. Those we interviewed, although not supportive of the Taliban or other insurgent groups, repeatedly cited as reasons for the decline in support civilian casualties, arbitrary detention and ill-treatment, intrusive house searches, the use of dogs against villagers, failure to admit and compensate for losses resulting from personal and property damage as well as from wrongful detention, and cultural insensitivities. Such conduct undermines the cooperation of civilians with the Afghan government and international troops and sends a message that foreign troops are at war with, rather than assisting, the Afghan people.

Under current ISAF counterinsurgency rules, foreign military forces, including U.S. forces that are part of the ISAF mission, must transfer detainees to Afghan custody within 96 hours. In contrast, under the OEF counterterrorism mission detainees captured by U.S. forces are transferred to Bagram for long-term detention, subsequently released, and since 2007 are transferred to Afghan custody for criminal prosecution in the U.S.-built Afghan National Defense Facility (ANDF) in Pul-e-Charkhi prison.

There are approximately 600 individuals being held in long-term detention by the United States in the Bagram Theater Internment Facility. Most are Afghans, but a small number are non-Afghans, including some who were captured outside Afghanistan and rendered to Bagram for detention. The BTIF will be replaced with a new theater internment facility in 2009.

In April 2009, Human Rights First interviewed former prisoners held by the United States in Afghanistan who at the time of their release were found by the U.S. military not to be a threat to U.S., Afghan or Coalition forces. Some detainees we interviewed had been detained for five years, others from four months to two years. According to those we interviewed in April, prisoners held by the U.S. military in Afghanistan were not informed of the reasons for their detention or the specific allegations against them. They were not provided with any evidence that would support claims that they are members of the Taliban, al Qaeda or supporters of other insurgent groups. They did not have lawyers. Detainees were not allowed to bring village elders or witnesses to speak on their behalf or allowed to offer evidence that the allegations could be based on individual animosities or tribal rivalries. These prisoners had no meaningful way to challenge their detention. Former prisoners and Afghan government officials told Human Rights First that captures based on unreliable information have led to the wrongful detention of many individuals, which in turn creates friction between the Afghan people and the Afghan government as well as the U.S. military.

In 2008 and in our follow-up visit to Afghanistan in 2009, we found that individuals transferred from U.S. to Afghan custody for prosecution in the Afghan National Defense Facility are tried in proceedings that fail to meet Afghan and international fair trial standards. Prosecutions were based on allegations and evidence provided by the United States, supplemented by investigations conducted by the Afghan intelligence agency, the National Directorate of Security (NDS), years after the initial capture. Although lawyers defend detainees at the ANDF, during the trials there were no prosecution witnesses, no out-of-court sworn prosecution witness statements, and little or no physical evidence presented to support the charges.

Human Rights First submitted its findings and recommendations to the Pentagon's Office of Detainee Affairs, U.S. Central Command (CENTCOM), and the President's Special Task Force on Detainee Disposition, created by Executive Order on January 22, 2009, which was tasked to identify "lawful options . . . with respect to the apprehension, detention, trial, transfer, release, or other disposition of individuals captured or apprehended in connection with armed conflicts and counterterrorism operations, and to identify such options as are consistent with the national security and foreign policy interests of the United States and the interests of justice."[4] In May 2009, at the time of our submissions to the government, we were aware that the Pentagon was revising detainee review procedures in Bagram and that broader detention reforms in Afghanistan were being considered. (For a detailed examination of our findings and recommendations see Human Rights First, *Undue Process: An Examination of the Detention and Trial of Bagram Detainees in Afghanistan in April 2009* (2009)).

Under the newly announced DRB procedures, detainees will have improved notification procedures, the ability to attend the hearings, call witnesses that are "reasonably available" and question government witnesses, and have a personal representative to assist them during the proceedings. If properly implemented, these procedures will certainly be an improvement over the quality of process afforded to Bagram detainees under the previous Unlawful Enemy Combatant Review Board (UECRB) procedures. On the other hand, similarities between the DRBs and the discredited Combatant Status Review Tribunals (CSRTs) in Guantanamo are cause for concern. Specific problems with the CSRTs that may also arise in the DRBs involve enforcement of detainees' entitlement to exculpatory information and their ability to review and challenge the evidence against them and produce their own evidence, including witnesses, all in the absence of entitlement to legal representation or independent review of their detention. It thus remains to be seen whether these new procedures go far enough to protect against arbitrary detention while also creating a sound evidentiary basis for fair prosecutions.

We are mindful that the United States, along with NATO allies and the Afghan government, is engaged in armed conflict with insurgent groups in Afghanistan and that detention is an element of armed conflict. But the United States should take additional steps to ensure an end to the arbitrary detentions that have undermined its counterinsurgency goals. U.S. counterinsurgency doctrine recognizes the benefits of consent from, and the need for cooperation of, the local population. A key determinant of that consent and cooperation is the degree to which the Afghan people view detention practices as fair, humane and beneficial to their security, and as progressively achieved through their own institutions. Reforms that accomplish these goals will deprive al Qaeda and the Taliban of the propaganda and recruiting opportunities created by unjust policies and practices.

Human Rights First urges further reforms to:

■ ensure that U.S. detentions are on a sound legal basis;

■ reduce the risk of arbitrary detentions by providing detainees a sufficient way to challenge their detention and improving evidentiary procedures at capture;

■ increase the transparency in U.S. detention operations;

- increase the capacity of the Afghan authorities to handle detentions on their own; and

- strengthen the fairness of Afghan criminal prosecutions of those captured by the United States.

Our recommendations to accomplish these reforms are outlined in detail at the end of this policy paper.

II. Detentions in Afghanistan

Authority to Detain

On September 14, 2009, the Pentagon unveiled a new policy guidance with modified procedures for reviewing the status of detainees being held in Afghanistan. The modified procedures follow the definitional framework of detention authority under the 2001 Authorization for Use of Military Force (AUMF) that the Obama administration adopted for Guantanamo detainees in March 2009.[5] Under this framework, U.S. forces operating under OEF can detain "unlawful enemy belligerents" (and no longer unlawful enemy combatants)[6] who meet the following criteria:

> Persons who planned, authorized, committed, or aided the terrorist attacks that occurred on September 11, 2001, and persons who harbored those responsible for those attacks;

> Persons who were part of, or substantially supported, Taliban or al-Qaida forces or associated forces that are engaged in hostilities against the United States or its coalition partners, including any person who has committed a belligerent act, or has directly supported hostilities, in aid of such enemy armed forces.[ ]

The policy guidance further instructs that:

> Internment must be linked to a determination that the person detained meets the criteria detailed above and that the internment is necessary to mitigate the threat the detainee poses, taking into account an assessment of the detainee's potential for rehabilitation, reconciliation, and eventual reintegration into society. If, at any point during the detainee review process, a person detained by OEF forces is determined not to meet the criteria detailed above or no longer to require internment to mitigate their threat, the person shall be released from DOD custody as soon as practicable. The fact that a detainee may have intelligence value, by itself, is not a basis for internment.[ ]

The new definition requires a demonstration of "substantial support" of Taliban or al Qaeda forces or associated forces engaged in hostilities against the United States and its coalition partners, while the previous criteria for capture and detention required only "support" of those forces. Some U.S. district courts that have evaluated this definition in Guantanamo habeas cases have rejected it as too broad.[9]

Passed by Congress in response to the 9/11 attacks, the AUMF authorizes the president to "use all necessary and appropriate force against those nations, organizations, or persons he determines planned, authorized, committed, or aided the terrorist attacks that occurred on September 11, 2001."[10] According to the government, because "the laws of war have evolved primarily in the context of international armed conflicts," the President has the authority to detain 'those persons whose relationship to al Qaeda or the Taliban would, in appropriately analogous circumstances in a traditional armed conflict, render them detainable."[11] While detention is an essential element in armed conflict, we submit that the AUMF—a U.S. domestic law—is an insufficient basis for detention by the United States in the current non-international armed conflict in Afghanistan.[12]

The international armed conflict between the United States and Afghanistan began on October 7, 2001, in response to the September 11 attacks, and concluded with the inauguration of Hamid Karzai on June 19, 2002, following his election by an Afghan *loya jirga*, to the presidency of the transitional administration of Afghanistan.[13] At this time, the hostilities involving international military forces and Afghan forces against the Taliban and al Qaeda became a non-international armed conflict (NIAC) governed by the international humanitarian law of NIAC, which is codified in Common Article 3 of the Geneva Conventions and Additional Protocol II.[14] The United States is no longer fighting the Afghan regime but is assisting the government in fighting insurgents in Afghanistan. The International Committee of the Red Cross (ICRC) has concluded that, since June 2002, the war in Afghanistan is a non-international armed conflict.[15]

The United States has consistently and publicly stated that "a central purpose of United States military operations in Afghanistan is to support the sovereignty of the Afghan state. That is true both for Operation Enduring Freedom . . . and for U.S. participation in the ISAF."[16] To advance this policy objective, and in the absence of a U.N. Security Council resolution explicitly authorizing long-term detentions by coalition forces in Afghanistan, the Afghan government as the host nation should either confer detention authority upon the United States through its domestic legislation or by way of a public U.S.-Afghan security agreement. Either must set forth grounds and procedures for detention in accordance with international law.

Reliance upon the AUMF to detain Afghan nationals not in the United States but in Afghanistan undercuts U.S. policy objectives to encourage increased responsibility of the Afghan government for its national security affairs. A public U.S.-Afghan security agreement or Afghan legislation would bolster U.S. support for Afghan sovereignty and advance U.S. strategy to progressively devolve responsibility for detentions to the Afghan government. The implementation of such legislation or an agreement regularizing U.S. detention would also advance the credibility of U.S. military actions in the eyes of Afghans, thus supporting U.S. counterinsurgency goals in Afghanistan.

Detainee Review Board Procedures

Detention is an essential element of armed conflict, but the grounds and procedures for detention must be consistent with international humanitarian law and the applicable standards of international human rights law. Common Article 3 and Additional Protocol II (AP II) do not provide procedural guidelines to govern reviews of detention in non-international armed conflicts. Thus it is necessary to refer to human rights law for guidance.[17] The ICRC has also developed a set of principles and safeguards which "reflect the official position of the ICRC" governing security detention in armed conflict and situations of violence.[18] The guidelines "are based on IHL, human rights treaties [such as the International Covenant of Civil and Political Rights], and human rights jurisprudence."[19] According to the guidelines, detainees in non-international armed conflict must have the right: to challenge the lawfulness of their detention, have an independent and impartial body decide on continued detention or release, to notice of charges, to a legal representative, to attend hearings, to have contact with family members, and to have access to medical care.[20]

Detainees held by the U.S. in Afghanistan since 2001 have had their status reviewed under various practices and procedures.[21] Beginning in 2007 and until September 2009, detentions in Bagram were reviewed by the Unlawful Enemy Combatant Review Board.[22] These procedures were an inadequate mechanism for detainees to meaningfully challenge their detention. In April 2009, Human Rights First interviewed former detainees who were released by the U.S. military after having been found to "no longer be a threat to U.S., Afghan or coalition forces." Interviewees consistently reported that no information was given to them about the grounds for detention, they had no ability to examine any information that supported the reason for detention, were not able to bring in witnesses to rebut the military's claims, and they had no knowledge of procedures or mechanisms to review of their detention. Detainees also complained of not having lawyers to assist them while in detention.[23] (*See generally* Human Rights

First, *Undue Process: An Examination of the Detention and Trial of Bagram Detainees in Afghanistan in April 2009* (2009)).

In April 2009, a district court judge ruling on habeas petitions filed on behalf of four detainees all of whom were allegedly captured outside Afghanistan and brought to Bagram for long-term detention concluded that UECRBs were "plainly less sophisticated and more error-prone" than the flawed CSRTs in Guantanamo. Judge Bates concluded that "the UECRB process at Bagram falls well short of what the Supreme Court [in *Boumediene v. Bush*] found inadequate at Guantánamo."[24] Judge Bates also expressed concern that a detainee has no "meaningful opportunity to rebut [the government's] evidence" and that the "ever-changing definition of enemy combatant, coupled with uncertain evidentiary standards, further undercut the reliability of the UECRB review."[25] Judge Bates held that non-Afghans captured Afghanistan and brought to Bagram had the right to habeas in U.S. courts.[26]

The new procedures made public and implemented in mid-September 2009 do address some of the complaints, but further reforms are needed to guard against arbitrary detention and allow detainees a more meaningful mechanism to challenge their detention as well as to make detentions more transparent and legitimate in the eyes of the Afghan people.

Under the new policy guidance, a Detainee Review Board replaced the Unlawful Enemy Combatant Review Board. The review board determines whether the person meets the criteria for initial detention, or continued detention, including whether he shall be released without conditions or transferred to Afghan authorities for criminal prosecution or participation in a reconciliation program.[27] For non-Afghans at Bagram, the review board can also recommend transfer to a third country for criminal prosecution, participation in a reconciliation program, or release.[28] Detainees currently in Bagram will have their status reviewed under the new DRBs when they come up for their already scheduled six-month review status determinations.

The new proceedings are an improvement from the UECRBs in the following areas:

- Under the new procedures a detainee's status is reviewed within 60 days, rather than 75 days, of a detainee's transfer to the BTIF and thereafter "at least every six months."

- The review board's report and recommendation will be in writing and will be reviewed for "legal sufficiency" by the office of the Staff Judge Advocate for the convening authority.

- Detainees will now be provided "timely notice of the basis for their internment" and provided an unclassified summary of facts that support the basis for their internment.

- Detainees will receive notice of the results of their review boards, in writing and orally, within seven days after completion of the "legal sufficiency review."

- Detainees will be able to present information and evidence and bring witnesses who are "reasonably available" either in person, through video or teleconference, or in a sworn statement.

- Detainees will be allowed to testify or address the review board and attend "open sessions, subject to operational concerns."

- Detainees will be assigned a personal representative to "assist the detainee in gathering and presenting the information reasonably available in the light most favorable to the detainee."

- If the review board decides that a detainee does not meet the criteria for internment, the detainee "shall" be released from DoD custody "as soon as practicable." Decisions to recommend internment, or transfer to Afghan authorities for criminal prosecution, or participation in a reconciliation program are subject to review by the convening authority.[29]

Although the DRBs are an improvement from the UECRBs, there are similarities between the DRBs and the discredited CSRTS. One of the lessons learned from the CSRTs is the potential for a gap between rules and their proper implementation. In Guantanamo, detainees' requests for witnesses were denied, decisions on detention were made largely on classified information which a detainee could not see, there was no confidentiality between the personal representative and a detainee, and the CSRT process by which a detainee's status was determined was subject to political interference. The Detainee Review Board procedures however, include several improvements to the CSRTs at Guantanamo as well. For instance, the DRB procedures do not presume the validity of the government's information as did the CSRTs. Unlike the CSRTs, a decision by the DRB that a detainee is not an "unlawful enemy belligerent" results in release and appears at least on paper to not be subject to further review by the convening authority. The DRB panel can also recommend a range of options for a detainee such as participation in a reconciliation program and where there is evidence of criminal conduct transfer to prosecution in Afghan courts.

Nevertheless, Human Rights First urges further reforms to detainee proceedings in Bagram in order to ensure that detainees have sufficient ability to challenge their detention and thereby guard against arbitrary detention. In particular, we have concerns in the following areas:

Information Relied Upon to Make Detention Decisions

The review board, comprised of field-grade military officers, will assess "all reasonably available information (including classified information relevant) to determine whether each person transferred to the BTIF meets the criteria for internment and, if so, whether the person's continued internment is necessary . . . to mitigate the threat the detainee poses."[30]

The guidance for the review board procedures however, fails to exclude evidence obtained through torture or cruel treatment in assessing initial or continued detention. This omission should be rectified immediately in order to confirm the stated intention of the Obama administration to make a clean break from past practices and policies that justified and excused detainee abuse.

Moreover, this exclusion is necessary in order to meet U.S. treaty obligations under article 15 of the Convention Against Torture, which prohibits statements obtained as a result of torture being used as evidence in any proceeding, except against a person accused of torture as evidence that the statement was made.[31] The use of information that has been obtained by torture or other cruel, inhuman or degrading treatment is antithetical to the rule of law. The Supreme Court has held that the rationale for excluding coerced statements is not just their unreliability; they should be inadmissible even if "statements contained in them may be independently established as true" because of the fundamental offence that coercive treatment of detainees causes to the notion of due process and the rule of law.[32]

The Pentagon should make every effort to break from past practices and policies and ensure that DRB determinations are not based on unreliable and coerced information.

Detainee's Ability to Confront Evidence

In contrast to the UECRB, the new procedures allow detainees to question witnesses called by the review board but subject to "any operational or national security concerns."[33] Detainees can also call witnesses "if reasonably available" and considered by the board to have "relevant testimony to offer." At the board president's discretion "relevant witnesses" may testify either in person, through video or teleconference, or in a sworn statement.[34] A similar provision applied to CSRTs in Guantanamo, but a Seton Hall Law School study of publicly available CSRT records found that even where a witness requested by a detainee was another detainee at Guantanamo, the CSRTs denied three quarters of such requests. And every request for witnesses not at Guantanamo was denied.[35]

Facilitating the presence of witnesses and exculpatory information is challenging, but given that detentions are in Afghanistan such requests should be processed more efficiently and should not be summarily dismissed as was the case with detainees being held at the U.S. naval base in Guantanamo Bay, Cuba and who requested evidence from their home countries or place of capture.

Under the DRB rules, detainees will not have access to classified evidence. Every effort should be made to avoid unnecessary classification, to declassify evidence or to separate classified sources and methods from substance, so that the review board does not rely exclusively on classified evidence. Detainees appearing before CSRTs were permitted to see unclassified evidence, but were unable to examine a majority of the evidence relied upon by the government in support of detention. The Seton Hall study found that the government relied exclusively on classified evidence in a majority of the cases.[36] The study concluded that at least 55 percent of the detainees asked to see classified evidence used against them or to present exculpatory evidence in the form of witnesses and/or documents.[37] Every request to review classified evidence was denied. In its brief to the U.S. Supreme Court in *Boumediene v. Bush*, the Bush Administration conceded that "in most cases" classified information "formed part of the basis for the government's determination that they were enemy combatants."[38]

Lack of Independence of the Review Board

According to ICRC guidelines, detainees should be able to challenge their detention before an independent and impartial body.[39] But the DRB procedures do not address the issue of lack of independence of the reviewing body. The guidelines note that to "ensure neutrality" of the review board, none of the review board members would

be "directly involved" in a detainee's capture or transfer to the BTIF.[40] But neutrality and independence are different. Independence goes to the lack of prejudice within the body and neutrality goes to the lack of outside influence.

The CSRT procedures in Guantanamo—which had similar provisions about the "neutrality" of the board—were fraught with the lack of independence and concerns about "command influence" and that a decision by the board was not binding. In a review of habeas cases, the Seton Hall CSRT Study showed that in at least three cases, detainees were initially found not to be "enemy combatants" but their cases were subjected to repeat CSRT proceedings without the presence of detainees and they were then found to be "enemy combatants."[41] A U.S. Army Major who sat on 49 CSRT panels, indicated that in six of these hearings "there was a unanimous decision that the detainee was a Non Enemy Combatant (NEC). In all of these NEC cases, the Command directed that a new CSRT be held or the original CSRT was ordered reopened. In each of those cases, the 'new evidence' that was presented was in fact a different conclusory intelligence finding, which was not justified by the underlying evidence."[42] The Major described command influence over the CSRT process, including in relation to cases of Uighur detainees. Some of these detainees had been found not to be "enemy combatants" while others had been affirmed as "enemy combatants" based on evidence that was essentially the same.[43]

In order to ensure independence of the proceedings, as well as to further the end goal of shifting detention authority to Afghanistan, the United States should involve Afghan judges—as they are not members of the detaining authority— in reviewing the detention of individuals held by the United States military. This also furthers U.S. strategy to build the capacity of the Afghan people to handle their own national security affairs.

Personal Representative and Not Legal Counsel

According to ICRC guidelines, detainees in non-international armed conflict should have the right to a legal representative when challenging their detention.[44] Under the DRBs, a personal representative will be assigned to each detainee to assist the detainee before the review board "not later than" thirty days prior to a detainee's hearing.[45] The military personal representative will have access to "all reasonably available information (including classified information) relevant to the determination of whether the detainee meets criteria for internment and whether the detainee's continued internment is necessary."[46] The personal representative is supposed to "act in the best interests of the detainee" and to "assist the detainee in gathering and presenting the information reasonably available in the light most favorable to the detainee."[47] The detainee may waive the appointment of such a representative, unless he is under eighteen years old or suffering from "a known mental illness," or is "determined by the convening authority" to be "incapable of understanding and participating meaningfully in the review scheme."[48]

A personal representative was appointed to each detainee for the CSRT process in Guantanamo. But a study of CSRT cases, found that in 78 per cent of cases, the detainee and his personal representative met only once, and in 91 per cent of these cases their meeting was less than two hours. In a third of cases, the meeting lasted for less than half an hour (this included the time needed for interpretation).[49] Moreover, there was no confidential relationship between the personal representative and the detainee in Guantanamo and the representative could relay to the CSRT any inculpatory information learned from the detainee.

The expectation that the personal representative will act in the best interest of the detainee, as would an attorney, is unreasonable given the inherently conflicting pressures faced by the representative due to his mission and place in the chain of command.

Criteria Used to Determine "Level of Threat"

Questions remain about what criteria is used to determine a detainee's "level of threat" to support detention. The guidance states that the review board will assess whether a detainee is an "Enduring Security Threat" which is defined in a separate guidance policy that is not public.[50] The guidelines further provide that the "Enduring Security Threat" is not a "legal category," but an "identification of the highest threat" a detainee poses for "purposes of transfer and release determinations." It is, however, unclear how this assessment is made and what mechanisms exist to ensure that "threat" assessments are not exaggerated or inflated. It is also unclear whether there is any place in the threat assessment process for consideration of the detriment to the overall U.S. mission that results from overbroad or vague grounds for detention.

III. Detention Reforms in Both U.S. and Afghan Prisons

In the summer of 2009, Major General Douglas Stone—who ran detainee operations in Iraq in 2007 and 2008 and initiated detainee reforms aimed at de-radicalization and faster processing—was sent to Afghanistan to assess U.S. and Afghan detentions and to report his findings to CENTCOM. In September 2009, General McChrystal's assessment on Afghanistan entitled "COMISAF Initial Assessment" was made public by the *Washington Post.*[51] Annex F, entitled *Detainee Operations, Rule of Law, and Afghan Corrections,* includes recommendations by Gen. Stone and outlines a series of reforms to both U.S. and Afghan detentions. Gen. McChyrstal states that "the long-term goal [is] getting the U.S. out of the detention business" and that the "desired endstate must be the eventual turnover of all detention operations in Afghanistan, to include the BTIF, to the Afghan government once they have developed the requisite sustainable capacity to run those systems properly."[52]

Human Rights First recognizes the significant challenges to accomplishment of this goal. There are serious problems with conditions of detention, treatment, and trials under Afghan authority. After thirty years of conflict, the formal Afghan justice sector is weak and faces serious difficulties, including poor infrastructure, inadequate training and education of lawyers and judges, lack of access to laws and textbooks, and corruption. International military troops are concerned that some individuals that they transferred to Afghan custody under ISAF rules were quickly released and re-engaging in anti-government activities. Individuals affiliated with the Taliban have broken out or bribed their way out of Afghan prisons.[53] There has also been lack of coordination between North Atlantic Treaty Organization (NATO) allies on rule of law reform. Human Rights First is also aware that prisons in Afghanistan play a role in radicalizing prisoners and recruiting people for the insurgency which further underscores the need to process prisoners expeditiously, house prisoners in humane conditions, separate hardline from petty criminals, ensure fair trials, and to institute vocational training programs to help reintegrate former prisoners who have served their sentence into society.

General McChyrstal's report notes that at the BTIF "due to a lack of capacity and capability, productive interrogations and detainee intelligence collection have been reduced. As a result, hundreds are held without charge or without a defined way out." [54] The report also raises concerns about an overcrowded Afghan Corrections System (ACS) where insurgents mingle with petty criminals, radicalize non-insurgent inmates and use the facilities to conduct operations against Afghan and coalition forces.[55]

Annex F of the report outlines some ways to address these concerns. The report recommends the creation of a new Combined Joint Interagency Task Force (CJIATF) to work towards the "long term goal of getting the U.S. out of the detention business" and to "build the capacity of the Afghan government to take responsibility of detention in its own country."[56] The CJIATF will assume "oversight responsibilities to support detention and interrogation operations of all U.S.-held detainees in Afghanistan and train and apply corrections management techniques" and "rule of law principles in all detentions."[57] In essence, before the U.S. turns over detention operations to Afghanistan, it will apply rule of law reforms to current detention regimes and engage in capacity building on the Afghan side to handle such detentions. The CJIATF is also tasked to design and implement programs to address de-radicalization, rehabilitation, vocational and technical training, and segregating detainee populations in both U.S. and Afghan prisons.[58]

General McChrystal's report recommends the creation of a "Legal Group" within the CJIATF to "identify gaps in the Rule of Law framework that are inhibiting U.S. and Afghan detention/corrections operations from completing their mission and will develop solutions through consistent engagement with GIRoA [Government of the Islamic Republic of Afghanistan] elements and the International Community."[59] The report also noted that ISAF will be training its forces to better collect intelligence and evidence for prosecution in the Afghan judicial system.[60] These important steps should take into account the evidentiary gaps that exist in current capture practices by both OEF and ISAF forces and hinder Afghan prosecutions.

Afghan defense lawyers and prosecutors have both expressed concerns to Human Rights First that there are problems with the evidence that is transferred with a detainee both by ISAF and OEF forces. On many occasions evidence is simply lacking or does not meet evidentiary requirements under Afghan criminal procedure. Human Rights First has observed trials of former Bagram prisoners at the ANDF where there are no prosecution witnesses or sworn statements, thereby depriving a defense counsel of the ability to challenge the evidence. Instead, a judge decides the fate of a prisoner based on a summary of unverified allegations that have largely been collected by international military forces and transferred to Afghan authorities. Such trials fail to meet both international and Afghan fair trial standards. (For examples, read Human Rights First, *Arbitrary Justice: Trials of Bagram and Guantanamo Detainees in Afghanistan* (2008)).

IV. Recommendations

General McChrystal's report concludes that there are "strategic vulnerabilities in a non-Afghan system . . . [of detention and that] an Afghan system reinforces their sense of sovereignty and responsibility."[61] Human Rights First agrees. To establish legitimacy in the eyes of the Afghan people and to more fully align U.S. detentions with strategic priorities, additional steps are needed now:

- to ensure that U.S. detentions are on a sound legal basis;

- to increase the capacity of the Afghan authorities to handle detentions on their own;

- to establish more transparency in U.S. detention operations;

- to reduce the risk of arbitrary detentions by providing detainees a sufficient way to challenge their detention and improving evidentiary procedures at capture; and

- to strengthen the fairness of Afghan criminal prosecutions of those captured by the United States.

To achieve these goals, Human Rights First makes the following recommendations for action by the U.S. and Afghan governments:

Increase Afghan Involvement and Provide Greater Transparency

To the United States and Afghan Governments:

The governments of Afghanistan and the United States should establish a transparent legal framework for the detention of those captured by the U.S. military in Afghanistan, either through a security agreement or Afghan legislation that sets forth the legal grounds for detention and the procedures for the review of detention and which meets the requirements of international humanitarian law and human rights law applicable to non-international armed conflict.

The Afghan government retains formal sovereignty over its territory, including with respect to persons detained by international military forces operating in Afghanistan. An appropriate, publicly declared legal framework established by the governments of the United States and Afghanistan is necessary to guard against arbitrary detention, ensure that both international and Afghan military forces operate within the rule of law, and bolster the credibility of those operations among the Afghan people and within the international community. In order to ensure wider support for such a detention scheme, any agreement or legislation should be approved by the Afghan National Assembly in accordance with article 90 of the Afghan Constitution.

To the U.S. Department of Defense:

Amend the Detainee Review Board (DRB) procedures to provide for joint U.S.-Afghan participation on the Board.

Implementing a joint U.S./Afghan detainee review body that includes participation by Afghan judges would begin to involve Afghan authorities in detainee review procedures. This would promote an Afghan justice system that complies with international standards, would enable Afghanistan to take some measure of responsibility for its own citizens and others on its territory, would add to the quantum of information upon which detention decisions are based, and would hopefully provide greater credibility to detention decisions among the Afghan population.

Although the new procedures suggest that the DRB panel will not be involved in the capture or apprehension of a detainee, efforts to increase Afghan participation can help insulate the DRB from command influence and ensure that the decision-making process is impartial and independent.

Ensure transparency in the Detainee Review Board procedures in order to promote credibility and to assess the effectiveness of the new procedures.

Facilitate observation of the detainee review board proceedings by Afghan and international human rights organizations and publicly make available the transcripts of DRB proceedings.

Grant human rights observers access to detainees and detention facilities in Afghanistan.

Human Rights First's research suggests that treatment of detainees at Bagram has improved since the implementation of the 2006 Army Field Manual and application of Common Article 3 to Afghanistan, yet independent human rights monitors are not permitted access to the detention facility and to detainees. International and Afghan-based human rights organizations, in particular the Afghan Independent Human Rights Commission (AIHRC), should be provided access to facilities where conflict-related detainees are held and should be allowed to meet with detainees privately so that a public, credible, and independent assessment can be made about conditions of confinement and interrogation techniques. Such access and reporting would set an example of transparency and inspire confidence that the U.S. is meeting its humane treatment obligations. Although the International Committee of the Red Cross (ICRC) does have access to the BTIF and to detainees, its findings are confidential and thus the public does not learn about conditions of confinement and treatment.

Reduce the Risk of Arbitrary Detentions

To the U.S. Department of Defense:

Amend the Detainee Review Board procedures to improve the ability of detainees to examine and challenge the evidence against them, exclude evidence gained through coercion, and create a combined repository of information.

- Amend the procedures to explicitly state that no evidence/information that is a result of coercion may be used by the review board to determine whether a detainee meets the criteria for initial detention, continued detention, or for referral to prosecution in Afghan courts.

- Ensure that classified evidence is not the exclusive or predominant form of information relied upon by the DRB in making its decisions about a detainee. Every effort should be made to assess what information can be declassified so as to facilitate its use by a detainee before the DRB or in the event of future prosecution in Afghan courts.

- The DRB proceedings provide for a "Legal Sufficiency Review" of the DRB's decisions by the Staff Judge Advocate. This review should include an accounting of all efforts to obtain exculpatory information requested by a detainee and a detailed explanation of the results of such requests. The results of this audit should be made available to every detainee who requests exculpatory evidence.

- It will advance the U.S. strategy in Afghanistan to ensure that the new DRB process is set up to examine the universe of intelligence and information that led to a detainee's capture, including a review/assessment of the inculpatory and exculpatory evidence and whether facts support detention, criminal prosecution, release, or rehabilitation and reconciliation. We therefore recommend creation of a "Combined Detainee Document Management System" that consists of records from every U.S. and

Afghan agency that has intelligence or information on a detainee—such as the Central Intelligence Agency, Department of Defense, Federal Bureau of Investigation, Department of Justice, National Security Agency, Department of State, Afghan National Directorate of Security, Afghan National Army, Afghan National Police, and the Afghan National Security Council. Such a document repository would allow the DRB to fully assess the universe of information/intelligence when making a decision. The detainee should be provided as much unclassified information as possible in order to effectively challenge the evidence against him and to request exculpatory evidence. For detainees imprisoned in Bagram for several years, the challenges to finding credible information are particularly great, and could be better met through the availability of a central data source.

Provide detainees with a legal representative.

Although it will require additional resources, detainees should be provided a legal representative rather than a non-lawyer personal representative. Lawyers are trained and ethically obligated to work in the best interests of their client. A lawyer would therefore have greater independence and would be more effective than a non-lawyer in identifying witnesses and gathering evidence to challenge the lawfulness of his or her client's detention. Moreover, the detainee's conversations with a lawyer will be confidential, which is not the case with a non-lawyer military representative.

Repatriate or transfer non-Afghans detained in Afghanistan.

The United States should stop rendering persons captured outside of Afghanistan to Bagram. All persons captured outside Afghanistan and brought to Afghanistan must be repatriated to their country of origin for release or prosecution unless there is sufficient evidence to support criminal prosecution in U.S. courts. Upon repatriating detainees, the United States should turn over all evidence in its possession, including exculpatory evidence.

Establish procedures at capture that reduce the risk of detention based on faulty intelligence and that facilitate fair decisions regarding detention or criminal prosecution.

■ For future captures, work with the government of Afghanistan to implement guidelines that minimize erroneous detention, loss of civilian life, and damage to property.

Operation Enduring Freedom (OEF) troops should develop and implement guidelines to authenticate intelligence that is used to justify raids and other military actions—working more closely with local communities, officials, and with Afghan National Security Forces (ANSF)[62]—in order to weed out faulty information based on personal or tribal animosities. OEF forces should also develop guidance for conducting operations that demonstrate respect for religious and cultural values and minimize damage to property during house searches and seizures.

■ Provide training and resources to implement reliable detainee documentation procedures at the point of capture.

In order to ensure that individuals are detained based on reliable information, soldiers and intelligence officers must be provided with proper training and support. Additional resources must be allocated to train soldiers and intelligence officers (including ANSF who may work with OEF forces) in collection and maintenance of information to support detention, mitigate risks of erroneous detentions or release of dangerous individuals due to insufficient evidence, and for future prosecution, if necessary.

According to the Pentagon's May 2008 Detainee Operations, Joint Publication 3-63 guidelines, capturing units are supplied with flex-cuffs, goggles, zip-lock bags, trash bags, duct tape and evidence/property custody document forms. The military leadership should seek JAG officer (Judge Advocate General) input regarding what additional supplies, such as cameras, markers, labels, rulers, etc., might be necessary to effectively collect evidence at the point of capture. Procedures to establish a chain of custody should be implemented.

- Soldiers should be required to write a sworn statement describing the circumstances and reasons for the capture. This may involve basic training as to what information is relevant, including but not limited to the name of the detainee, the point of capture, evidence found with the detainee, witness names, and the reason for capture, including whether it was based on an intelligence source.

- The intake officer at a Forward Operating Base (FOB), or any other detention facility, should be a lawyer or, at a minimum, a paralegal who should examine whether all evidence has been properly identified and whether the sworn statement is complete.

- Intelligence officers who are involved in identifying a potential suspect for capture should be required to record the reasons in support of capture. Reasonable measures should be taken to protect the identity of informants. Efforts should be made to assess what information can be declassified so as to facilitate its use in prosecutions where warranted. This information should be included in the detainee's file as he is processed through the system.63

Increase Capacity for Fair Criminal Trials in Afghan Courts

To the U.S. Department of Defense:

Establish a new task force to improve the quality of evidence collected by U.S. troops and identify improvements in due process for cases transferred by the United States for criminal prosecution in Afghan courts.

- After finding evidentiary and due process failures in Afghan courts, Human Rights First recommended in its April 2008 report Arbitrary Justice: Trials of Bagram and Guantanamo Detainees in Afghanistan that the Pentagon create a legal task force to facilitate fair

prosecutions of individuals in Afghan courts. We recommended that this task force should work to improve the quality of information and evidence that is collected by U.S. forces and transferred to Afghan authorities. (The U.S. military's Task Force 134 in Iraq reportedly assisted with documentation of evidence and prosecution of insurgents in the Central Criminal Court of Iraq. JAG officers trained soldiers and marines to collect evidence for criminal prosecution in Iraqi courts. U.S. soldiers also appeared as witnesses in Iraqi courts, sometimes through video teleconference.64) We continue to stress that proper documentation of evidence and source information by intelligence officers and soldiers will lead to more reliable and fair prosecutions of detainees, reduce the risk of releasing dangerous prisoners due to insufficient evidence, and minimize the risk of detaining innocents.

- The "Legal Group" created under Combined Joint Interagency Task Force (CJIATF) should be provided with the necessary resources to facilitate fair prosecutions and should include Afghan lawyers to ensure that evidentiary standards under Afghan law are met in preparing files for prosecutions in the Afghan justice system.

To the Afghan Supreme Court and the Ministry of Justice

Direct judges presiding over the Afghan National Defense Facility (ANDF) trials to comply with the Afghan criminal procedure code, Afghan constitution, and international fair trial standards. Specifically, the Afghan courts in these cases should:

- Ensure that defense counsel has access to all information that will be relied upon by the prosecution during trial.

- Require in-court witness testimony and allow cross-examination of witnesses by defense counsel.

To the ANDF Review Committee and the Afghan Attorney General

- Notify defense counsel prior to the questioning of his client by the investigator and prosecutor and allow defense to be present during his client's questioning as mandated by the Afghan criminal procedure code.

- Request eye witness testimony or out-of-court sworn statements from U.S. and Afghan officials conducting detainee investigations and make available the information to defense counsel.

- Respect and enforce the decision of the highest court of Afghanistan after it has confirmed the acquittal of a defendant by permitting the release of the defendant.

V. Conclusion

Further reforms in U.S. detentions practices as well as continuing investment in a strengthened Afghan justice system will foster better relations with the Afghan population and advance the U.S. strategic mission to grow the capacity of Afghans to provide for their own security. The detention reforms unveiled by the Obama administration if properly implemented are an improvement in U.S. detention policies. But further reforms are needed to ensure that detention operations are under an appropriate legal framework and that detainees have a meaningful way to challenge their detention consistent with international law and U.S. policy to support and respect the sovereignty of Afghanistan and build the capacity of the Afghan authorities to take responsibility for detention operations. Moreover, by implementing better detainee documentation and evidence collection procedures in situations of armed conflict the United States would guard against the detention of innocent individuals and unfair prosecution of those tried in Afghan courts. Respect for the rights of Afghan citizens is not only important to defeat the insurgency, but is also a necessary precondition to establishing long-term stability in Afghanistan through the rule of law.

VI. Endnotes

[1] COMISAF's Initial Assessment, Initial United States Forces-Afghanistan (USFOR-A) Assessment, August 30, 2009, Annex F, p. F-1.

[2] *White Paper of the Interagency Policy Group's Report on U.S. Policy toward Afghanistan and Pakistan*, March 2009, http://www.whitehouse.gov/assets/documents/Afghanistan-Pakistan_White_Paper.pdf

[3] The poll concluded that in 2005, 83 percent of Afghans had a favorable opinion of the United States but in 2009 just 47 percent hold that view. And 25 percent say attacks on U.S. forces or International Security Assistance Force (ISAF) can be justified, up from 13 percent in 2006. While 25 percent of Afghans say violence against U.S. or other Western forces can be justified, this number jumps to 44 percent among those who report coalition bombing, raids or shelling in the area. ABC News/BBC/ARD Poll, "Support for U.S. Efforts Plummets Amid Afghanistan's Ongoing Strife," February 9, 2009, http://abcnews.go.com/images/PollingUnit/1083a1Afghanistan2009.pdf.

[4] Executive Order No. 13,493, *Review of Detention Policy Options* (January 22, 2009).

[5] *In re Guantánamo Bay Detainee Litigation*, No. 08-442, Respondents' Memorandum Regarding the Government's Detention Authority Relative to Detainees Held at Guantánamo Bay (D.D.C. March 13, 2009).

[6] Under the OEF counterterrorism mission launched in 2001, and up till September 2009, U.S. forces could detain "unlawful enemy combatants" in order to: "[Prevent] them from returning to the battlefield and [deny] the enemy the fighters needed to conduct further attacks and perpetrate hostilities against innocent civilians U.S. and coalition forces, and the Government of Afghanistan. The United States also gathers important intelligence from the unlawful enemy combatants during their detention, which in turn enables the United States to prevent future attacks." (*Bakri v. Bush*, No. 1:08-1307, Declaration of Colonel Charles A. Tennison, dated September 15, 2008, submitted in support of Respondents' Motion to Dismiss ("Tennison Declaration"), ¶9.). A September 2006 Pentagon directive defined "unlawful enemy combatant" as: "[P]ersons not entitled to combatant immunity, who engage in acts against the United States or its coalition partners in violation of the laws and customs of war during an armed conflict. For purposes of the war on terrorism, the term Unlawful Enemy Combatant is defined to include, but is not limited to, an individual who is or was part of or supporting Taliban or al Qaeda forces or associated forces that are engaged in hostilities against the United States or its coalition partners." (U.S. Department of Defense, The Department of Defense Detainee Program, Directive 2310.01E (Sept. 5, 2006), p. 9).

[7] Detainee Review Board Procedures at Bagram Theater Internment Facility (BTIF), Afghanistan, attached as an appendix to Brief of Respondent-Appellants appeal to the U.S. Court of Appeals for the District of Columbia, *Maqaleh v. Gates*, Nos. 09-5265, 09-5266, 09-5277 (D.C. Cir. Sept. 14, 2009) ("2009 DRB Procedures").

[8] Ibid.

[9] *See, e.g., Hamlily v. Obama*, 616 F. Supp. 2d 63, 69, 76 (D.D.C. 2009) (The Court "rejects the concept of 'substantial support' as an independent basis for detention . . . [and] finds that 'directly support[ing] hostilities' is not a proper basis for detention. In short, the Court can find no authority in domestic law or the law of war, nor can the government point to any, to justify the concept of 'support' as a valid ground for detention." The Court elaborated: "After repeated attempts by the Court to elicit a more definitive justification for the 'substantial support' concept in the law of war, it became clear that the government has none. Nevertheless, the government asserted that 'substantial support' is intended to cover those individuals 'who are not technically part of al Qaeda,' but who have some meaningful connection to the organization by, for example, providing financing. . . . . [A] detention authority that sweeps so broadly is simply beyond what the law of war will support."); *Gherebi v. Obama*, 609 F. Supp. 2d 43, 71 (D.D.C. 2009) (interpreting "substantial support" to include individuals who were actual members of enemy organizations' armed forces); *Anam v. Obama*, No. 04-1194, 2009 WL 2917034, at 2 (D.D.C. Sept. 14, 2009) (adopting *Hamlily* ruling).

[10] Authorization for Use of Military Force, Pub. L. No. 107-40, 115 Stat. 224 (2001).

[11] *In re Guantánamo Bay Detainee Litigation, supra* note 9.

[12] The Supreme Court in 2006 in *Hamdan v. Rumsfeld* rejected the Bush administration's argument that the conflict with al Qaeda is an international armed conflict based on a reasoning that international armed conflict can only be between states and that non-international armed conflict can only

occur within the territory of a single state. Instead, the court appeared to conclude that that the conflict with al Qaeda in Afghanistan is a non-international armed conflict as understood for the application of Common Article 3. 548 U.S. 557, 628-631 (2006).

[13] According to the Bonn Agreement, art. 1: "An Interim Authority shall be established upon the official transfer of power on 22 December 2001. . . ." Art. 3: "Upon the official transfer of power, the Interim Authority shall be the repository of Afghan sovereignty, with immediate effect." *See Agreement on Provisional Arrangements in Afghanistan Pending the Re-Establishment of Permanent Government Institutions* (December 5, 2001).

[14] Although neither the United States nor Afghanistan is a party to AP II, much of its content is widely deemed to be customary international humanitarian law. *See also* Jean-Marie Henckaerts and Louise Doswald-Beck, *Customary International Humanitarian Law*, International Committee of the Red Cross (Cambridge Univ. Press, 2005), vol. 1 (the ICRC's authoritative iteration of customary IHL).

[15] International Committee of the Red Cross, "International humanitarian law and terrorism: questions and answers," May 5, 2004, http://coe-dmha.org/TAPpdfs/IIIMEF2006/Resource%20Materials/International%20Law/IHL%20docs/Handbooks,%20Guidance%20references/IHL%20&%20Terrorism.pdf.

[16] *Maqaleh v. Gates*, No. 09-5265, Brief for Respondents-Appellants, (D.C. Cir. Sept.14, 2009), pp. 39-40.

[17] The preamble to Additional Protocol II establishes the link between AP II and human rights law by stating that "international instruments relating to human rights law offer a basic protection to the human rights." The United States and Afghanistan are both parties to the International Covenant of Civil and Political Rights (ICCPR), which prohibits arbitrary detention and mandates court review of any detention. Article 9(4) of the ICCPR states: "Anyone who is deprived of his liberty by arrest or detention shall be entitled to take proceedings before a court, in order that that court may decide without delay on the lawfulness of his detention and order his release if the detention is not lawful."

[18] The ICRC has stated that Common Article 3 and Additional Protocol II "provide no further guidance on what procedure is to be applied in cases of internment . . .[thus] the gap must be filled by reference to applicable human rights law and domestic law, given that international humanitarian law (IHL) rules applicable in non-international armed conflict constitute a safety net that is supplemented by the provisions of these bodies of law." *See* International Committee of the Red Cross, International Humanitarian Law and the Challenges of Contemporary Armed Conflicts, 30th International Conference of the Red Cross and Red Crescent (Geneva: November 2007), p. 11 ("2007 ICRC IHL Conference") and Jelena Pejic, Procedural Principles and Safeguards for Internment/Administrative Detention in Armed Conflict and Other Situations of Violence, 87 International Review of the Red Cross 375 (2005).

[19] Pejic, *Procedural Principles and Safeguards*, *supra* note 18, pp. 384-390.

[20] Ibid.

[21] According to the U.S. periodic report submitted to the Committee against Torture in 2005, the review process for detainees prior to the UECRB was as follows: "Detainees under DoD control in Afghanistan are subject to a review process that first determines whether an individual is an enemy combatant. The detaining Combatant Commander, or designee, shall review the initial determination that the detainee is an enemy combatant. This review is based on all available and relevant information available on the date of the review and may be subject to further review based upon newly discovered evidence or information. The Commander will review the initial determination that the detainee is an enemy combatant within 90 days from the time that a detainee comes under DoD control. After the initial 90-day status review, the detaining combatant commander, on an annual basis, is required to reassess the status of each detainee. Detainees assessed to be enemy combatants under this process remain under DoD control until they no longer present a threat. The review process is conducted under the authority of the Commander, U.S. Central Command (USCENTCOM). If, as a result of the periodic Enemy Combatant status review (90-day or annual), a detaining combatant commander concludes that a detainee no longer meets the definition of an enemy combatant, the detainee is released." *Update to Annex One of the Second Periodic Report of the United States of America to the Committee Against Torture* (May 2005), available at http://www.state.gov/g/drl/rls/55712.htm

[22] According to a November 2006 affidavit of Col. Rose Miller, Commander of Detention Operations in Bagram, the review board was called "Enemy Combatant Review Board" (ECRB) and consisted of five commissioned officers who evaluated a detainee's status. The change to UECRB occurred sometime in 2007 and now comprises of three officers rather than five. *Ruzatullah v. Rumsfeld*, No. 07-CV-07107 (D.D.C. Nov. 19, 2006).

[23] According to Col. Charles Tennison, the Commander of Detention Operations in 2008, Combined Joint Task Force 101, a detainee in Bagram under the UECRB was "notified of the general basis of his detention within the first two weeks of in-processing. . . . [b]arring operational requirements." A review of a detainee's status in Bagram was "usually conducted" within seventy-five days of detention and every six months thereafter. The UECRB, comprised of three commissioned officers, assessed a detainee's status and by majority vote recommended to the Commanding General or his designee that a detainee either be released or remain in detention. The UECRB reviewed information from a "variety of sources, including classified intelligence and testimony from individuals involved in the capture and interrogation of the detainee." Since April 2008, detainees being screened for the first time had an opportunity to appear before the UECRB for their initial review and make written submissions in subsequent reviews. The "implementing guidance" for UECRBs and the documentation prepared for UECRB evaluations of detainees were, and remain classified. *See generally* Tennison Declaration, *supra* note 6.

[24] *Maqaleh v. Gates*, No. 06-1669, Memorandum Opinion, (D.D.C. Apr. 2, 2009).

[25] Ibid.

[26] *Ibid*. On April 2, 2009, Judge Bates, applying the test articulated in the landmark Supreme Court case in *Boumediene v. Bush*, which recognized habeas rights for Guantánamo detainees, ruled that three non-Afghan detainees captured outside Afghanistan and brought to Bagram can challenge the lawfulness of their detention in U.S. federal courts. In the case of Afghan petitioner Haji Wazir, Judge Bates concluded that there was a "possibility of friction with Afghanistan" should Wazir obtain habeas review in U.S. courts. Judge Bates delayed his ruling on the case until further arguments could be made by the parties. On June 26, Judge Bates affirmed the motion to dismiss Haji Wazir's petition. The case is under appeal in the Court of Appeals in the District of Columbia.

[27] 2009 DRB Procedures, *supra* note 7, p. 4.

[28] Ibid.

[29] *See generally* 2009 DRB procedures, *supra* note 7, pp. 1-6.

[30] Ibid., pp. 1-2.

[31] Convention Against Torture and Other Cruel, Inhuman or Degrading Treatment or Punishment, 1465 U.N.T.S. 85, art. 15. The treaty was ratified by the United States in 1994.

[32] *Rochin v. California* 342 U.S. 165 (1952).

[33] Ibid.

[34] 2009 DRB Procedures, *supra* note 7, p. 3-4.

[35] Mark Denbeaux & Joshua Denbeaux, *No-Hearing Hearings, CSRT: the Modern Habeas Corpus? An Analysis of the Proceedings of the Government's Combatant Status Review Tribunals at Guantanamo* (2006), pp. 2-3 (hereinafter "No-Hearing Hearings").

[36] Ibid.

[37] Ibid.

[38] *Boumediene v. Bush*, No. 06-1195, Brief for the respondents, in the U.S. Supreme Court, (Oct. 2007).

[39] Pejic, *Procedural Principles and Safeguards*, *supra* note 18, pp. 384-390.

[40] Ibid.

[41] *No-Hearing Hearings*, *supra* note 35, p. 37.

[42] *Hamad v. Gates*, No. 07-1098, Response to omnibus motion to stay orders to file certified index of record, (D.C Cir. Oct. 4, 2007), Exhibit A.

[43] Ibid.

[44] Pejic, *Procedural Principles and Safeguards*, *supra* note 18, pp. 384-390.

[45] 2009 DRB Procedures, *supra* note 7, p. 3.

[46] Ibid., p. 5.

[47] Ibid., p. 6.

[48] Ibid.

[49] *No Hearing Hearings*, *supra* note 35, pp. 14-18.

[50] 2009 DRB Procedures, *supra* note 7, p. 5.

[51] COMISAF's Initial Assessment, *supra* note 1, p. F-1.

[52] Ibid. Annex F, p. F-2.

[53] Sam Yousufazai and Ron Moreau, "Afghan Prison Blues," *Newsweek*, February 11, 2008 (describing how Taliban members bribed their way out of NDS custody); Sami Yousafzai, "Inside the Prison Escape," *Newsweek*, June 30, 2008 (describing how Taliban fighters and other prisoners broke out of Sarposa prison in Kandahar which had 15-20 men crammed in tiny cells and allowed inmates to pay $100 a month to possess mobile phones); Hamid Shalizi, "Knives, Petrol Bombs Found in Afghan Prisons," *Reuters*, July 5, 2008. (describing how Afghan security forces found knives, petrol bombs, and mobile phones in Pul-e-Charkhi prison outside of Kabul).

[54] COMISAF's Initial Assessment, *supra* note 1, p. F-1.

[55] Ibid.

[56] Ibid., p. F-1-F-2.

[57] Ibid., p. F-2

[58] Ibid. In September 2009, the Pentagon announced the creation of Joint Task Force 435 – Operation Enduring Freedom (JTF 435), - whose Deputy Commander, Brig. Gen. Mark Martins is tasked to: "provide care and custody for detainees, oversee detainee review processes and reconciliation programs, and to ensure U.S. detainee operations in Afghanistan are aligned effectively with Afghan criminal justice efforts to support the overall strategy of defeating the Taliban insurgents." Mark Seibel, "Task Force Created to Combat Al Qaeda in Afghan Prisons," *McClatchy Newspapers*, October 1, 2009.

[59] COMISAF's Initial Assessment, *supra* note 1, p. F-3.

[60] Ibid., p. 2-18.

[61] Ibid. p. 2-16.

[62] The ANSF includes Afghan National Army (ANA), Afghan National Police (ANP), and Afghan National Army Air Corps (ANAAC).

[63] These recommendations are based on conversations with former JAG officers who served in Iraq.

[64] *See* Major W. James Annexstad, "The Detention and Prosecution of Insurgents and Other Non-Traditional Combatants—A Look at the Task Force 134 Process and Future of Detainee Prosecutions," *Army Lawyer*, July 2007. Human Rights First has not examined the trials at CCCI and cannot attest to the fairness of the proceedings. Nor have we examined the adequacy of the investigations to build a criminal case by Task Force 134. The comparison to Task Force 134 is to show that the U.S. military has engaged in evidence gathering and has made soldiers available for testimony in Iraqi criminal trials of persons captured by the United States.

www.ingramcontent.com/pod-product-compliance
Lightning Source LLC
Chambersburg PA
CBHW051422200326
41520CB00023B/7332